The Diverse Schools Dilemma

A Parent's Guide to Socioeconomically Mixed Public Schools

Michael J. Petrilli

Thomas B. Fordham Institute • November 2012

Published by the Thomas B. Fordham Institute
1016 16th Street NW, 8th Floor
Washington, D.C. 20036
www.edexcellence.net
(202) 223-5452

The Thomas B. Fordham Institute is the nation's leader in advancing educational
excellence for every child through quality research, analysis, and commentary, as well as
on-the-ground action and advocacy in Ohio. It is affiliated with the Thomas B. Fordham
Foundation, and this publication is a joint project of the Foundation and the Institute.
For further information, please visit our website at www.edexcellence.net or write to the
Institute at 1016 16th St. NW, 8th Floor, Washington, D.C. 20036. The Institute is neither
connected with nor sponsored by Fordham University.

ISBN: 978-0-615-65233-7

Text set in Minion Pro
Cover art by Joe Portnoy
Design by Alton Creative, Inc.
Printed and bound by Chroma Graphics

9 8 7 6 5 4 3 2

For Meghan

Contents

Introduction

Heather Schoell, a white, college-educated, stay-at-home mom living in the Capitol Hill neighborhood of Washington, D.C., was incredulous when a friend suggested that she should send her daughter to the local public school. "Honestly, I was like, 'Right, D.C. Public Schools—we're not even looking at that,'" Schoell recalled later.[1] Maury Elementary wasn't much to look at; its drab 1960s-era building had opaque, yellowing windows that made the place feel desolate. One hundred percent of its students were African American, most of them from low-income families. Schoell pictured mayhem behind those dreary windows, poor kids just running around. But her friend, who had volunteered at the school for twenty-five years, continued to press her, saying, "Give it a chance, go inside and see."

So she did, when her daughter was two and a half. And what she saw wasn't at all what she'd imagined. The principal at the time, a military veteran, exuded a confidence that put many of Schoell's concerns to rest. The school was disciplined, teachers had high expectations for students, and the administration was eager to welcome new students.

Schoell was relieved to find that the school might be a real possibility. She and her husband couldn't afford private school. And the couple, both raised in rural communities, refused to decamp to the suburbs. "We chose to come to D.C. because it was pretty much the antithesis of where we grew up," she said. "We want our kids to have the benefits of everything that the city has to offer."

Around the same time Schoell visited Maury, in 2005, a group of mostly white parents was pushing the school system to start a preschool program there for three-year-old children. Capitol Hill was experiencing a baby boom, and there weren't enough spots at local preschools to go around. A city councilman got involved, and by the fall a publicly funded program for three-year-olds was off the ground.

This was the beginning of a transformation at Maury, starting with its youngest students. Whereas the upper grades at the school had just one classroom apiece—all of which were 100 percent black—within a few years the three-year-old program had four classrooms that were racially and socioeconomically mixed. Maury is now an integrated school, to the pleasure, Schoell says, of everyone involved.

Maury's hopeful story is part of a larger trend. In the middle of the last decade, in urban communities across America, middle-class and upper-middle-class parents started sending their children to public schools again—schools that for decades had served overwhelmingly poor and minority populations. From Schoell's Washington neighborhood to northwest Denver, to Brooklyn, and beyond, white families in particular have come back to local schools—not in dribs and drabs but in droves. In one D.C. high school, students sarcastically called it "the Caucasian invasion."

One big reason for the shift has been gyrations in the housing market. As prices rose dramatically in the 1990s and the early 2000s, up-and-coming neighborhoods that young families might have previously avoided now stood as their best chance for affordable urban housing. (Thanks to the sharp drop in crime, these neighborhoods were safer than ever before, too.) Many of these folks, progressive-minded members of the "creative class" that Richard Florida made famous, chose urban or close-in suburban communities full of art galleries, trendy coffee shops . . . and lousy schools.[2]

When the market crashed, lots of these young parents found themselves underwater on their starter homes and frozen in place. Even those with equity realized that, with tighter credit and tougher lending guidelines, they couldn't afford to move anywhere much more expensive, and they were forced to start thinking about making their urban lives work for the long term. Plenty had come to love living in cities and, like Heather Schoell, refused to make the trek to the bland 'burbs. Unable to afford going private, they had to contemplate their local public schools.

My wife and I can relate. After we married and started thinking of having a baby, we sought a suitable, stroller-friendly neighborhood in or around Washington, D.C. It couldn't be too expensive; at the time I worked for the government, and my wife was soon to become a stay-at-home mom. I insisted on a house with a yard, but neither of us wanted to move far from the city. That's where we worked and played, and a bikeable commute downtown was a must. Early in our home search we stumbled across Takoma Park, Maryland, a diverse community adjacent to D.C. that's renowned for its crunchy, hippy vibe. (It's often called "the People's Republic" or "Berkeley East.") We fell in love with the bungalows and Victorians and the lush tree canopy, and found ourselves amused by the organic food co-op, the folk festival, the strident political activism, and the earnest environmentalism. We found an adorable (read: very small) 1920s cottage bungalow on a street packed with little kids, and bought in.

When our first son was born, we came to appreciate Takoma Park even more. Like other inner suburbs and leafy city neighborhoods we know, it's toddler heaven. Partly that's because of the plentiful parks. But mostly it's because of the easy walks. We could stroll to the library for story time, to friends' homes for playtime, to the local co-op to pick up milk, to the Sunday farmer's market, or to the Metro station to visit downtown museums. There was a real sense of community—a rarity in so much of modern America.

Still, we weren't sure we wanted to stay in Takoma Park for the long term. Mainly, we were concerned about its schools. They have a mixed reputation and lackluster test scores, largely due to their diverse population of students. (Research has long shown that poor and minority students tend to perform worse on standardized tests than affluent white children.[3]) At our local elementary school, white students were a minority, and one-third of the kids were poor enough to qualify for free or reduced-price lunch from the federal government.

We very much liked the idea of our son becoming friends with kids from other races and backgrounds, and we didn't think we could afford private school. But we expected that our boy would be entering kindergarten with the basics—and more—under his belt, and we worried he wouldn't get the attention and challenge he needed. What if his teachers were focused on helping recent immigrant children learn English, or giving low-income kids remedial help? What if the schools were test-prep factories, obsessed only with getting students to basic proficiency in reading and math? After six years in our Takoma Park house, with our older son reaching preschool age and his little brother on the way, we started wondering if we should move again, to a more affluent, less diverse suburb like Bethesda, Maryland, where these sorts of issues wouldn't be a factor.

If we knew that our kids would do just as well in a diverse school in Takoma Park and be just as safe, we'd stay, no question. We would have it all: a great education in an environment that reflects the world they are going to live in.

On the other hand, if there was clear evidence that our kids would do better in homogeneous schools, there would be no question either. None of us would knowingly put our children in harm's way, or curtail their opportunities to learn. Just as we wouldn't move our family into a dangerous housing project to promote the cause of social justice, we wouldn't send our children to a school with kids from that same project if we thought we were risking their safety.

This book will argue that the truth is somewhere in between. While there are clear benefits for affluent students who attend diverse schools, there are also clear risks. The question that each of us must answer for ourselves is whether the former outweigh the latter.

■ ■ ■

This book is for parents, like my wife and me, who are grappling with the Diverse Schools Dilemma. Middle-class or upper-middle-class Gen-X and Gen-Y parents like us embrace the idea of our children living, learning, and playing side by side with kids from other cultures and economic backgrounds. But we worry about the potential costs. Will diverse schools be academically challenging for all of their students? Safe? Well-rounded, with lots of time for art and music, exploration and play? Not obsessed with test scores? Will they prepare our kids to get into a good college? I wanted to know the answers to these and other questions—and writing this book gave me an excuse to find out. And as an education policy wonk (my day job is helping to lead the Thomas B. Fordham Institute, an education reform think tank), I had access to research and experts that others might not.

It's likely that you're holding this book and thinking about diverse public schools for your kids, because that's what your own neighborhood has to offer. Maybe you're an urban pioneer living in a gentrifying part of the city, or a dweller of the inner-ring suburbs, the prime location where America's full diversity can be found.

You might be a parent looking for a home, and realizing that the urban neighborhoods that are both affordable and desirable come with diverse schools. In fact, the diversity is largely what *makes* those neighborhoods affordable—they have public schools that many well-off parents wouldn't even consider.

This book will help you determine whether a diverse public school might work for you and your family. We'll explore questions like these: How do middle-class students perform in these schools? What special challenges do diverse schools present? What kind of academic programs and enrichment activities can you find in schools like these? Why are so few "progressive" schools racially and economically mixed? How much socioeconomic diversity is too much?

You are making an incredibly important decision on behalf of your children. Is selecting a diverse public school a responsible choice, or an unreasonable risk?

■ ■ ■

Let's be clear: This question doesn't even come up for the vast majority of white, middle-class families. Eighty-seven percent of white students attend majority-white schools, even though white children make up just over 50 percent of the U.S. public school population. And just 14 percent of white students attend "multicultural" schools—those where three racial groups each make up at least 10 percent of the population.[4]

This shouldn't be surprising to anyone who has been paying attention to demographic shifts in recent years. As analysts such as Bill Bishop (in *The Big Sort*) or Rich Benjamin (in *Searching for Whitopia*) have illustrated, many middle-class whites, especially those who are more conservative, have moved beyond the boundaries of the suburbs into the vast communities of the exurbs. And no doubt this is partly to find "good schools"—code for (let's be frank) those without too many poor or minority kids.

But progressive-minded parents contribute to segregation, too. Almost every metropolitan area has at least one affluent, progressive enclave with mostly white public schools. Think of Newton, Massachusetts; Beverly Hills and Marin County, California; Scarsdale, New York; or Bellevue, Washington. In the D.C. area, it's the aforementioned Bethesda. Its state legislative district went 74–25 for Barack Obama in 2008, and it boasts five Whole Foods stores within a twenty-minute drive. Several of its schools serve virtually no poor students and very few African American or Hispanic children.

Take Wood Acres Elementary School. Its attendance zone votes over-whelmingly Democratic; less than 1 percent of students are low-income, 2 percent are black, and 5 percent are Hispanic. It's hard to get much richer or whiter than that.

It's not like the houses in the Wood Acres area are all gold-plated man-sions. Even modest brick colonials sell in the upper six figures. Part of what's happening there (and in similar neighborhoods nationwide) is that people are paying a premium to send their kids to homogeneous upper-middle-class schools—or "private public schools," as I once labeled them.[5]

The good news is that if you are willing to send your kid to a diverse school—better yet, if you *want* to send your kid to a diverse school—you should be able to get a bigger or nicer house than you could otherwise afford. And in a cool urban neighborhood to boot!

But don't expect accolades from family and friends. I spoke with Annette Lareau, a renowned sociologist who is studying the differences between middle-class parents who stay in the city and those who bolt for the suburbs. (We'll examine her groundbreaking work on differing parenting styles in Chapter Three.) The suburban parents she has interviewed get basically no pushback about their decision to flee the city. They tell Lareau, "We had kids, were moving to the area, and asked people where to live. Everyone pointed here. They said the schools were great." These parents didn't put a whole lot of thought into it beyond that. They could talk to Lareau for a half hour about the ins and outs of the local soccer program or the evils of sugar, but they had only hazy memories of how they settled on their neighborhood, or whether they checked out the schools (even online) before making their decision.

The middle-class parents who decided to send their kids to diverse urban schools, on the other hand, are constantly "called to account for their decision," Lareau told me. "People say it's not in their children's best interests. They are seen as compromising their children's life chances, and are questioned by families, co-workers, and even neighbors."

■ ■ ■

The first half of this book will examine the pros and cons of socioeconomically diverse public schools. The second half will present some potential solutions to the Diverse Schools Dilemma. We'll explore how to find a great diverse public school, school choice options (including charter and magnet schools), the phenomenon of schools (like Maury Elementary) that are experiencing dramatic demographic changes, and, for those who can afford it, the decision to go private.

And in the epilogue, I'll share my own family's answer to the Diverse Schools Dilemma. No fair reading ahead to see how the story ends!

Endnotes

1   Where not cited, quotations are drawn from personal interviews with the author.

2   See Richard Florida's books on the "creative class," including *The Rise of the Creative Class: And How It's Transforming Work, Leisure, Community, and Everyday Life* (New York: Basic Books, 2003) and *The Flight of the Creative Class: The New Global Competition for Talent* (New York: HarperBusiness, 2005).

3   See Chapter One of this book for a discussion of the achievement of poor and minority students versus affluent white students.

4   Gary Orfield, *Reviving the Goal of an Integrated Society: A 21st Century Challenge* (Los Angeles: UCLA Civil Rights Project, 2009).

5   See Michael J. Petrilli and Janie Scull, *Private Public Schools* (Washington, D.C.: Thomas B. Fordham Institute, February 2010), http://www.edexcellence.net/publications/americas-private-public.html.

1

The Case for Saying "Yes" to Diverse Public Schools

If you're like me, and you're honest with yourself, you'll find plenty of reasons to say no to a school with a lot of socioeconomic diversity. Maybe you are worried your son or daughter won't be safe, or sufficiently challenged and engaged.

So why say yes? As I wrote in the introduction, there are plenty of selfish reasons to choose urban schools like these: You can usually buy a bigger house and be closer to work and cultural activities. As Alan Berube, a friend and an urban policy expert at the Brookings Institution told me, "My wife and I like living [on Capitol Hill] because, yes, it's diverse, but also because it's near the Metro, it has relatively easy access to amenities, and because the housing is cheaper than a lot of other parts of D.C. (and inner suburbs like Bethesda), which leaves us more room in our budget to do other things we like."

Or maybe it's guilt. Perhaps you watched *The Colbert Report* after conservatives in Wake County, North Carolina, ended a busing program designed to create socioeconomically integrated schools. "What's the use of living in a gated community," Colbert deadpanned, "if my kids go to school and get *poor* all over them?"[1]

Self-interest and guilt aside, there are noble reasons for choosing diverse schools: Doing so may make our society better, and it may make our children better.

School Segregation: A Short History

It's impossible to discuss issues of school diversity without considering the historical context. For a succinct, stirring examination of school segregation and desegregation, it's hard to beat sociologist Gerald Grant's recent book, *Hope and Despair in the American City*. Grant, whose father worked at a butcher shop and a steel mill and whose mother grew up in an orphanage, was raised in a working-class neighborhood in Syracuse, New York. As young parents, he and his wife Judy were progressives who "saw the suburbs as bland, sterile Levittowns, or as pretentious subdivisions that would gradually sprout McMansions—places without a sense of history or soul that were destroying the rural landscape and befouling the air with endless commuting."[2]

And yet, after living in cosmopolitan neighborhoods in Washington and Boston, the couple settled in a suburban community twenty miles from Grant's old stomping grounds in Syracuse. Grant explains why:

> By the time I became a professor at Syracuse University in 1972, all our children were in grade school. We decided to choose a school first and a house second. We began our search in city neighborhoods near the university. But in school after school, we felt we were being processed by a bureaucracy rather than welcomed as future parents. Worse, especially for my wife—a progressive educator who had founded the Lowell School in Washington, which placed a high value on the arts and creative play—the schools we visited were dispiriting. In the one we liked best, all the pictures lining the hallway were nearly identical turkeys that the children had colored inside the lines. Judy's classroom visits confirmed her feeling that the teaching was as stilted and unimaginative as the turkeys.[3]

Soon after, the Grants stumbled upon a charming suburban village on Skaneateles Lake, with idyllic public schools—but virtually no black residents. With many mixed feelings, they bought in. And the Grant family enjoyed their years there—swimming in the lake in the summer, walking to school, taking pottery lessons from neighbors. Six years later, Judy had an opportunity to teach in a Syracuse city school with a new, visionary principal. There was just one hitch: School employees had to reside in the city. After much thought and discussion, they said yes.

The Grants bought a home in Syracuse's diverse Westcott neighborhood. There was much they loved about their new life. "Westcott's location seemed to meet our needs perfectly," Grant wrote. "Judy and I could have a dinner party and then drive to Symphony Hall or Syracuse Stage in five minutes. I enjoyed the walk to my campus office, overlooking the city from the hills in Thornden Park."[4]

Yet all was not well with the neighborhood, or with Syracuse in general. White flight, which peaked in the 1960s and '70s, was taking its toll; by 2000 Syracuse had lost 40 percent of its population. That included most of the city's civil servants—its teachers, police officers, and firefighters. (It turned out that the residency requirement for city employees was rarely enforced and later scrapped.) As the population declined, crime and disorder increased. White suburbs thrived, while mostly black Syracuse started a long death spiral. This was a story being played out in cities across America. Grant wrote:

> In urban environments like Syracuse, opportunity shrank and pathology deepened for children in ways that suburban children would never know. The concentration of poverty and unemployment led to a loss of authority in schools and more incivility on the streets. Networks of support were much more deeply frayed in city neighborhoods, and in some they virtually collapsed.[5]

The Grants got involved with heroic efforts to save their neighborhood and revitalize its schools—efforts that "slowed the exodus and even drew some young families to Westcott," Grant wrote. Still, he admitted, "there was a net loss of social capital."[6] Reformers couldn't counteract the larger forces that were pulling most of the affluent and well-educated parents out of Syracuse toward the suburbs.

As Grant explained, these forces were originally put into motion by Uncle Sam. First there were discriminatory housing policies, whereby neighborhoods with large proportions of black residents were redlined by federal mortgage appraisers and insurance companies. With loans more expensive in those communities, whites who could afford to go elsewhere had incentive to do so. Covenants in white neighborhoods barred minorities from moving in. After World War II, the Federal Housing Administration followed racist practices when backing mortgages for veterans under the GI Bill. Its policies allowed white families to purchase new homes in the suburbs with just 10 percent down, at very attractive interest rates, while stable, older, mixed-race neighborhoods with good-quality housing were rated as bigger risks, and borrowers there encountered much tougher terms.

The Supreme Court barred racial housing covenants in 1948, but covert redlining went on for decades. Suburban home buyers continued to receive preferential mortgage terms and insurance, while city homes continued to be undervalued. Add to this mix new interstate highways—which made long-distance commuting feasible for the first time, and also destroyed many urban neighborhoods—and you can see how all the incentives were pushing white families to the 'burbs.

These suburbs were perfectly engineered to keep poor families out. Suburban towns started to incorporate in the late 1800s as a way to avoid annexation by larger cities and to control their own fates. They put zoning ordinances in place that restricted or barred the creation of affordable housing, particularly apartment buildings. And they stopped public transportation initiatives that would have made it possible for poorer, carless families to live in their neighborhoods.

By the late 1970s, most American metropolitan areas exhibited a "donut hole" pattern: A mostly black city at the center was surrounded by a ring of mostly white suburbs. And as went the neighborhoods, so went their schools: black and white students, at least in the North and Midwest, were less likely than ever before to attend school together.

The Great Busing Wars

In 1954, *Brown vs. Board of Education* demanded that southern schools be desegregated with "all deliberate speed"—yet many states and school districts deliberately dragged their feet. It wasn't until the mid- to late 1960s, when Congress linked federal education aid to progress on desegregation, that *Brown*'s mandate was followed and southern districts were actually integrated.

Then things moved swiftly; by 1970, black students in the South were actually more likely to attend racially integrated schools than their counterparts in the North.[7]

This created a sticky situation for the courts; northern states had never put explicit laws in place mandating separate schools for black and white children. However, as Grant wrote, there was plenty of evidence that school districts had acted to keep black and whites in different schools, through decisions regarding school attendance boundaries and the like. (Discriminatory housing policies also led to residential segregation, which was even greater in the North than in the South.) In 1973, the Supreme Court for the first time ordered a city not in the South—Denver—to desegregate its schools. Soon many cities came under similar court orders—and because most neighborhoods in those cities were segregated by race, that meant busing on an unprecedented scale.

To say this led to massive resistance on the part of whites would be an enormous understatement. And no city epitomized this resistance more than Boston. The prelude, drama, and aftermath of Boston's busing battles are stirringly portrayed in J. Anthony Lukas's masterful book *Common Ground: A Turbulent Decade in the Lives of Three American Families*, which won a Pulitzer Prize in 1986. Lukas is careful to humanize all the parties in the busing debate—the African American families who wanted better opportunities for their kids, the poor whites (mostly Irish) who saw busing as a threat to their neighborhoods and way of life, and the affluent whites (mostly white Anglo-Saxon Protestants, or WASPs) who were quick to judge their less-wealthy peers, but whose own schools were as white as ever.

The reason that Boston's affluent whites could outrun school desegregation is that it stopped at the city line. That, according to Gerald Grant, was because of a "tragic" 1974 Supreme Court decision in which five justices refused to mandate interdistrict busing in Detroit and other northern cities.

The die was cast: Whites could stay in the city, watch their property values erode, see their children bused across town, and struggle with increasing crime; or they could get a cheap mortgage for a new house in a safe suburban neighborhood with "good" schools. For most, that wasn't a difficult decision.

By the 1990s, the courts declared most city school systems "unitary"—meaning they had removed the last vestiges of discrimination. But that didn't mean schools were integrated; rather, urban districts had lost almost all of their white students, so the courts had to admit that desegregation was no longer feasible. The city schools were "racially balanced" only in the sense that all of them had similar proportions of minority children: close to 100 percent.

How Segregated Schools Harm Poor and Minority Kids

For more than fifty years, throughout these great desegregation battles, social scientists tried to answer a simple question: Does how much you are likely to learn depend on who is sitting next to you in class?

While the evils of forced segregation are obvious to us today, in *Brown vs. Board of Education* the plaintiffs had to prove that segregating black children into separate schools was harmful to their development. It wasn't enough to show that they received unequal treatment, in terms of the condition of their school buildings, the quality of their books, or the training of their teachers. Because civil rights attorneys were seeking to overturn *Plessy vs. Ferguson*'s "separate but equal" doctrine, they had to demonstrate that even if school conditions were equal (which of course they weren't), black children still suffered from being concentrated in separate, all-black schools.

Sophisticated research studies examining segregation and student achievement weren't available yet, so lawyers relied on expert testimony about the harm segregation did to black children's self-esteem. While this evidence would be considered flimsy by today's social science standards, it was enough to convince a unanimous court to issue its landmark decision.

As the years passed, more compelling evidence emerged showing that a student's peers do make a big difference for his or her achievement. One of the first, and most important, studies to demonstrate this link was the famous 1966 Coleman Report, the result of an enormous federal research initiative headed by the late James Coleman, then a sociologist at Johns Hopkins University. He and his team gathered reams of data, including students' test scores and information about their families, teachers, schools, and more.

He expected to find a connection between school spending and student test scores. But he didn't. Instead, he discovered an overwhelming correlation between students' family background and their achievement. The wealthier the students and the better educated their parents, the higher they tended to score on tests. Adding resources to schools did little or nothing to lessen this relationship.[8]

Coleman uncovered another relationship that was almost as strong: Poor students learned more in middle-class schools than they did in schools with high concentrations of poverty. "Children from a given family background, when put in schools of different social compositions, will achieve at quite different levels," he wrote.[9] Other research has since confirmed this finding. And it's not just about test scores. One paper showed that minority students who had attended racially segregated schools were less likely to be employed in white-collar professional jobs when they got older, probably because they failed to make the social contacts that would later enable them to find meaningful work and because they hadn't learned how to navigate middle-class culture. Another study found that children who attended poor schools were three to four times more likely to live in poverty as adults than were similar children who attended middle-class schools.[10]

Still, skeptics dispute that this evidence proves the impact of peers. How can we be certain that it's the student composition of the school that is making such a difference, and not something else? Maybe students learn more in middle-class schools not because of their middle-class peers, but because the schools themselves are good. And because they are good schools, well-educated and well-informed middle-class parents flock to them.

Or maybe what's being detected isn't the effects of peers but of teachers—the best teachers avoid high-poverty schools, and that's why students do worse in those settings. If we could just figure out how to attract better teachers into poor schools, maybe their students would perform as well as pupils in middle-class schools.

Or perhaps the poor or minority children whose parents find ways to get them into white, middle-class schools are different in some immeasurable respect from poor or minority kids who end up in high-poverty, all-minority schools—creating a problem of "selection bias" in the research.

A newer study attempts to address that particular question head on. It examines a longtime "inclusionary housing" program in Montgomery County, Maryland, whereby new subdivisions or condominiums must set aside a number of units for low-income families. Families enter a lottery to move from the poorer parts of the county to more affluent areas. The study, by Heather Schwartz of the RAND Corporation, compared families who won the lottery to those who lost. She found that poor children who moved to socioeconomically integrated neighborhoods, and attended socioeconomically integrated schools, outperformed their peers by significant margins. About two-thirds of the difference was due to the schools, not the neighborhoods.[11]

So are peers making an impact? Disentangling the various factors is hard, but in recent years scholars have used increasingly sophisticated methods to do so. In 2000, Caroline Hoxby, a brilliant Stanford economist and Rhodes Scholar, published a paper examining peer effects in Texas schools. Her study used several innovative methods to deal with the selection-bias issue. She looked for random instances when the racial and gender composition of a cohort of students was significantly different from an adjacent cohort (for instance, this year's third graders compared to this year's fourth graders). Then she determined whether those differences had an impact on student achievement.

They did. Cohorts with larger proportions of girls made greater progress in reading and math, for example. (This is particularly interesting since boys generally outperform girls in math.) And cohorts with a larger proportion of black students performed worse than others; black students in particular lagged behind when more of their peers were black. Hoxby found a similar (though less pronounced) dynamic for Hispanic students—as the percentage of Hispanic students increased, their scores generally went down.[12]

The well-known education economist Eric Hanushek picked up on Hoxby's strand of work in a paper coauthored by John Kain and Steven Rivkin and published in 2009. He came to similar conclusions. Also studying achievement and segregation in Texas, he found that "black enrollment share adversely affects achievement, and the effects are roughly twice as large for blacks as for whites." In other words, as the percentage of black students goes up, the achievement of all students—but especially black students—goes down.[13]

A third, fascinating study is worth mentioning, too. This one, by economists Scott Imberman, Adriana Kugler, and Bruce Sacerdote, examined the fallout from Hurricanes Rita and Katrina. The authors wanted to know what happened when students who were evacuated from New Orleans ended up in schools in Houston. Their findings were consistent with the other research: The arrival of low-achieving evacuees, most of them extremely poor, dragged down the average performance of the native Houston students, while high-achieving evacuees had a positive impact on Houston students. Perhaps most intriguingly, disruptive evacuees also encouraged native students to misbehave at higher rates.[14]

Why Peers Matter

Richard Kahlenberg, a scholar at the liberal Century Foundation and one of the nation's premier authorities on school integration, makes a compelling case that classmates exert an enormous influence on one another. Few of us would doubt the power of peer pressure, especially for adolescents. As Kahlenberg points out, teenagers are more likely to smoke if their friends do, regardless of whether their parents smoke; and kids dress to impress their friends, not their elders. And when children raised by nannies and sent to boarding schools adopt their families' upper-class social mores, it is not because they are influenced by their parents, but because they are picking up cues from their peers, who are from the same social group.[15]

So it stands to reason that children and teenagers will also adopt their classmates' values about education. Plenty of studies show that middle-class children, in Kahlenberg's words, "place greater value on working hard and doing well academically" than poor children do. Some believe that this is largely an issue of race—black students are afraid of "acting white" by doing well in school. (More about that in Chapter Six.) But Kahlenberg insists that this difference has more to do with socioeconomic class—that "poor people of all races are more likely to cut classes, miss school, and do less homework."[16]

That's the problem President Barack Obama tackled head on when he gave a back-to-school address in the fall of 2009. "At the end of the day," he told the nation's students, "the circumstances of your life—what you look like, where you come from, how much money you have, what you've got going on at home—that's no excuse for neglecting your homework or having a bad attitude. That's no excuse for talking back to your teacher, or cutting class, or dropping out of school. That's no excuse for not trying."[17]

Yet a lot of kids attending high-poverty schools don't seem to be trying. It may be that they've already experienced a lot of failure and frustration in their early schooling. Or the lack of effort may reflect meager aspirations. "In low-income schools," Kahlenberg writes, "students ask one another, 'Are you going to college?'; in wealthier schools, the question is 'What college are you going to?'"[18] Poor children tend to have lower expectations for their own academic careers and job prospects than middle-class children do. And when they are surrounded exclusively by other poor kids, such low expectations get reinforced.

So the values and aspirations of students rub off on one another. But a child's classmates influence him in other ways that are much more direct. First, students do learn from one another. This isn't just in group settings where higher-achieving children are instructed to tutor lower-achieving ones. More importantly, students can pick up vocabulary from other kids—and virtually nothing is more important to the learning process than developing a large vocabulary. Poor children tend to have much smaller vocabularies when they enter school than middle-class children do—half as large, by some estimates. If poor and middle-class students go to school together, the former have a chance to pick up more vocabulary from the latter. But if poor kids are segregated into schools of their own, their vocabulary development is stunted.

Jane Cooley, a University of Wisconsin economist who studies peer effects and desegregation, offers another model for how students might be impacting their peers: by the questions they ask. "A teacher has a given amount of time," she told me. "Even a child asking questions in class is taking time away from others. Being with a kid that asks better questions would positively affect learning."

Students also influence one another's learning through behavior. It's hard to learn in a class that's constantly being interrupted by kids who are acting out. Remember the Hoxby study that found that cohorts with more girls learned more than cohorts with more boys, even though on average boys do better at math? She hypothesized that the issue came down to classroom discipline. Little boys tend to misbehave more than little girls, and this misbehavior probably had a negative impact on everyone's learning.

Such disruptions are much more common in high-poverty schools, which also experience more violence, vandalism, theft, and other problems. And there's some evidence that bad behavior can be contagious. In the Katrina study, low-achieving Houston natives were particularly susceptible to the influence of low-achieving, misbehaving New Orleans transplants. It wasn't just that some of the Katrina refugees were behaving badly. They encouraged other kids to do so, too.

The Power of Parents

So kids influence one another—that should come as no surprise. What's not so obvious, though, is how parents can also impact a child's classmates. Kahlenberg argues that this happens in two important ways. First, having more parents volunteer in the classroom raises the achievement of all kids— even those whose parents aren't there. This likely reflects the existence at the school of greater "social capital," a concept popularized by James Coleman. What this means is that strong social networks can add tremendous value— in schools, civil society, markets—that enhance productivity and efficiency.

Schools with strong ties among parents, teachers, and students develop social capital that can benefit the entire school community. When more parents volunteer in a school, positive relationships are built among parents and between parents and staff. More adults are around to help kids. And a common sense of responsibility for all the children develops that might extend beyond the walls of the school.

Active parents can also help all students in a school by pressuring administrators to address problems and work toward continuous improvement, and by pushing for a school to get its fair share of resources. Lackluster teachers, crummy facilities, and mediocre curricular materials all are more likely to be rectified in schools with a critical mass of involved, confident, pushy parents.[19]

Poor parents are much less likely to be actively involved in their children's schools, struggling as they are with working two or three jobs and putting food on the table, or perhaps having had bad relationships with schools themselves when they were kids. So most schools that are predominantly poor see few volunteers and feel minimal pressure from parents to improve. In short, they have less social capital. When a school is socioeconomically diverse, there's a silver lining: All kids—including the poor ones—can benefit from the positive impact of the middle-class parents who are most likely to pitch in.

"The Very Students Who Need the Most Get the Least"

All else being equal, students who are poor perform better when they attend schools with significant numbers of middle-class children. Students who are black or Hispanic perform better when they attend schools with significant numbers of white children. And students who are low-achieving perform better when they attend schools with significant numbers of high-achieving children. Is it any wonder that so many social scientists supported the cause of school desegregation, even in the face of fierce political opposition?

But the story is even starker, because "all else" is hardly equal.

It's no secret that schools in this country are funded unfairly. According to the liberal advocacy group Education Trust, the school districts with high proportions of minority students receive $1,100 less per pupil annually in state and local funds than districts that serve predominantly white and Asian children.[20] Inequities within school districts can be even greater. An analysis by University of Washington researcher Marguerite Roza demonstrated that districts like Austin, Texas, were spending up to $400,000 more in their most affluent schools than in their poorest ones—enough to hire at least six additional teachers.[21]

It's true that researchers as far back as the Coleman Report have failed to find a reliable link between spending and student outcomes. Still, it's hard to justify giving fewer resources to the schools facing the greatest challenges. As Kati Haycock, the head of Education Trust, has said, "The very students who need the most get the least."

One factor drives such disparities more than anything else, and it does matter to student achievement: teachers. One of the most consistent findings in education is that teacher quality is tremendously important. For example, Eric Hanushek found that in a single school year, a good teacher can move a student's achievement a full grade level higher than a bad teacher can.[22] Think about that: Your first grader could be on either a second-grade level or a third-grade level by the end of the year—just because of the quality of her teacher.

By all traditional measures, the most qualified teachers are clustered in the most affluent, whitest schools.[23] Those teachers tend to score higher on certification exams and are more likely to have majored in the subjects they teach. They also tend to be more experienced, and since virtually all U.S. school systems pay teachers based on years of experience and degrees earned, rather than on how good they are, this means they earn higher salaries than their newer colleagues do.

It's this concentration of veteran teachers in the most affluent schools that drives the inequities in school spending, at least within districts. For example, teachers in Austin's most affluent schools earn almost $4,000 more, on average, than teachers in its poorest schools, who tend to be younger. Each school might have the same number of teachers, yet the system is spending a lot more on educating its wealthiest students than its poorest.

Many veteran teachers simply prefer teaching in affluent schools, where students are better prepared to learn, support from parents is higher, violence and disruptions are rarer, and life is generally easier. Because senior teachers usually have first dibs on open jobs in a school system, they take the best positions at the most attractive schools before new hires even have a shot at them. And why not? They generally don't get paid any more to stay at the toughest schools.

Here's how it works: A new teacher gets hired right out of college and placed in one of the system's poorest schools. He or she works for several years, improving his or her skills dramatically. (Teachers are typically much more effective after two to three years in the classroom.) Then a position opens up across town, in a more affluent setting, and the teacher bolts. The cycle starts all over again, with another rookie teacher hired to teach in the poorest school.

Teachers practice on poor children, then take their improved skills to affluent children—and our system abets this. Why? Think about what would happen in an urban school district if the superintendent proposed taking the best teachers from the wealthy side of town and sending them to the schools in poor neighborhoods. Rich parents would scream bloody murder and pressure the school board to overturn the decision or get rid of the superintendent. These parents—who tend to be relentless—know how to work the system to get resources for their schools. And why shouldn't they? They love their children. So do poor parents, but they are no match politically in this battle for resources and responsiveness.

Maybe the best teachers simply don't want to work in poor neighborhoods because they are distant from their homes, or because they feel unsafe. Or perhaps some teachers are attracted or repelled by particular schools because of their student demographics. This isn't pleasant to imagine, but it may be true. C. Kirabo Jackson, a labor economist at Cornell University, studied the Charlotte-Mecklenburg, North Carolina, school system in 2002–03, the year the district ended its long-standing desegregation program. Almost overnight, the student composition of Charlotte's schools changed dramatically, as both white and black students retreated back to their neighborhood schools. Interestingly, if depressingly, Jackson found that teachers moved, too. Schools that saw an influx of black students saw an outflow of their most effective teachers (both black and white).[24]

The neighborhoods didn't change. Teachers' commutes didn't change. The only thing that changed was the students. As a result, teacher talent moved toward whiter, more affluent, and higher-achieving schools, and away from blacker, poorer, struggling ones.

The rich got richer and the poor got poorer, no doubt about it. Separate was definitely not equal.

Can't We Fix High-Poverty Schools?

It should be clear by now that segregating poor, minority, or low-achieving children into separate schools is unhelpful for their educational and life prospects. But must it be?

Many education reformers, on both the right and left, think the answer is no. In fact, the issue of school segregation is rarely mentioned nowadays within policy circles. Many policy wonks believe that we tried desegregation and it failed, because whites moved to the suburbs and away from the reach of court-ordered busing. If large-scale social engineering is impossible or undesirable, they say, let's get on with the business of making poor inner-city schools work.

That's the intent of all the major strands of education reform, which include efforts to drive extra dollars to the neediest schools, raise academic standards and expectations for students, implement dramatic turn-around strategies in low-performing schools, attract talented teachers to poor schools via financial and other incentives, and create greater competition and choice within the public education system. That's the intent of President George W. Bush's No Child Left Behind law, as well as President Obama's Race to the Top education policy agenda.

Yet the sobering truth is that none of these efforts—nor similar ones going back twenty-five years—has been very successful. While demography need not be destiny, reforms to date have been generally ineffective at severing the link between advantage and achievement. Identifying high-achieving schools with a high concentration of poor or minority kids is like finding needles in a haystack.

Consider the research of Douglas Harris, a University of Wisconsin economist. He dug into a massive database of school test scores and demographics and found that just 1 percent of high-poverty schools place in the top third of student achievement.[25] Still, that 1 percent means there is hope. Some of these exemplars are celebrated widely, and appropriately so. Many of the most famous are charter schools, which are public schools parents can choose that operate outside of traditional school systems and teacher union contracts and thus have more freedom to innovate. President Obama is strongly supportive of charter schools, and Secretary of Education Arne Duncan has used his clout to push states to pass charter-friendly legislation.

One model that charter supporters love to point to is KIPP: the Knowledge is Power Program. This national network now includes 109 schools in twenty states and the District of Columbia, which serve more than 33,000 students. It's been the subject of massive media attention, from *The Oprah Winfrey Show* to *60 Minutes* to Malcolm Gladwell's *Outliers*. Most KIPP schools serve predominantly poor populations, almost entirely African American and Hispanic, yet they generally achieve dramatic results.

Many of KIPP's approaches hold promise for other poor schools. The schools create a strong culture that's obsessive about getting kids to graduate from college. They use innovative (some would say heavy-handed) discipline methods. They teach a rich, challenging curriculum. And, perhaps most importantly, they attract phenomenally talented, committed teachers who regularly work sixty hours or more a week on behalf of their students.

But there's a big debate about the meaning of KIPP for the larger education reform movement. For one, KIPP has only about one hundred schools. Even if you throw in the few hundred other urban charter schools that are similar to KIPP, they still make up a tiny share of the 100,000 schools in the United States today. Perhaps all of these high-achieving charters combined serve 100,000 students—about the same as one large urban district. And there are approximately 20 million students in America poor enough to qualify for free or reduced-price lunch, so KIPP and its ilk would have to multiply fifty times over to serve even a quarter of them.

There are some people who wouldn't want to see KIPP grow like that. Some analysts think KIPP and its counterparts "cream" the highest-achieving, most motivated, best-parented students from neighborhood schools. This creaming could occur in a number of ways. First, parents must proactively choose these schools, so they have to be informed and motivated enough to enroll their children in the first place. (KIPP tries to overcome this barrier by walking city blocks and knocking on doors.) Second, parents have to sign contracts promising to support their children's education, which could dissuade some from participating. Third, a big chunk of KIPP students—as many as 60 percent in one Bay Area KIPP school—drop out and return to their traditional public schools.[26] The kids who stay at KIPP tend to be the higher achievers.

KIPP's backers argue that KIPP students are just as poor as their peers in neighborhood schools, which is generally true. But it's certainly possible that KIPP parents are more likely to be strivers who are particularly committed to seeing their children get a great education and go to college. I don't say this to diminish KIPP and it counterparts. In providing very effective environments for promising poor kids to learn at high levels, they are providing an incredibly important service. Together, these charter schools will dramatically boost the number of poor and minority kids going to college, which is a huge contribution. But if it is true that KIPP's success relies in part on the nature of the people who choose it, then most high-poverty schools would be unlikely to replicate KIPP's results. In that case, a different strategy—integrating our schools—is worth trying, too.

The Benefits of Diversity for Your Children

So that's the moral and social-justice case for choosing a diverse school. But what about the more parochial case? How could enrollment in a school with lots of poor children help to build the character and skills of your kids?

I posed that question to Secretary of Education Arne Duncan, whose children have attended racially and socioeconomically integrated schools in Chicago and Northern Virginia. "It's so cliché," he responded, "but it's so important that young children grow up around folks who are different from them—kids with different backgrounds, different socioeconomic status, different languages. I think the benefits of that are incalculable, and however successful you are academically and intellectually, without that I think you put a real ceiling or limit on what you can accomplish long-term if you're not absolutely comfortable and confident in that kind of setting."

Perhaps the most relentless spokesperson for diverse schools is Gary Orfield, a UCLA professor who has led the push for school integration for forty years as the head of the Civil Rights Project. He isn't just an advocate; he walked the walk by putting his own children in a mostly poor, mostly black elementary school on Capitol Hill when he lived in Washington, and then sent them to public schools when he resided in Chicago's Hyde Park neighborhood.

I called Orfield to get his expert perspective on the issue of school diversity, but he mostly wanted to talk about his kids. He described their achievements with evident pride: Two graduated from top-tier law schools, and another is a professional ballerina. They are also, in his words, "fluently multicultural." They know how to cross boundaries of race, class, and culture because of the environments in which they grew up. This gives them great advantages, he argued, because the ability to understand and connect with individuals from other cultures is essential for anyone who wants to excel at a top-tier university, in a challenging career, and in twenty-first-century America more generally.

"Too many middle- and upper-class whites are trying to protect their kids from experiences and challenges that would actually be very interesting and stimulating to them," Orfield wrote me after our talk. These experiences would "much better prepare them to be part of a successful minority in the extremely diverse society of the American future."

Eileen Kugler, a mother and the author of *Debunking the Middle-Class Myth: Why Diverse Schools are Good for All Kids,* made a similar case: "If you try to protect your children from every potentially 'disturbing' aspect of life," she wrote me, "they will never develop the resilience to deal with the real issues they face as adults. It is of great benefit for them to interact with kids who are poor, or who have just arrived from another country and don't speak English well, or who have dealt with the issues of racism, to gain some insights on how life really is. Life is complex, and the more our children understand that, the better they will be in dealing with the complexities of their lives when they grow up."

Amy Stuart Wells, a well-known professor at Columbia University's Teachers College, reiterated this argument. She led a team of scholars that interviewed over 500 people who graduated from high school in 1980, all of whom participated in desegregation programs. (These interviews were conducted between 1999 and 2004, when the graduates were in their late 30s and early 40s.[27]) These adults told Wells and her colleagues that going to diverse schools was "essential to their success in a global economy and increasingly diverse society." Wells told me, "There's a boundary crossing that you learn when you go to a school that's diverse. The white students especially learn to be comfortable in any setting, even when they are in the racial minority."

Consider, too, the views of Rhiana Maidenberg, a mom, former teacher, and freelance writer living in San Francisco. In an article for the website Babble she explained her decision to send her daughter to public school. She admitted that she's concerned that the school system doesn't offer frequent art, music, and gym classes. But, she reasoned, "The main thing private schools can't provide that public schools can is diversity. The experiences my kids will receive in a classroom filled with children of varying backgrounds, native languages, and races will help them grow to be well-rounded world citizens. While I can make up for a lack of music class, if we chose private school, I couldn't enroll them in diversity training."[28]

These arguments are persuasive, yet anecdotal. Thankfully, there is some hard evidence that diversity benefits middle-class youngsters. Two quantitative studies from the 1990s—one of Oklahoma whites, and the other of college students—found that the more frequently children interacted with kids of other races, and the more positive those interactions were, the less likely they would grow up to be prejudiced as adults.[29]

That's the case for saying "yes" to diverse public schools. Now let's explore the case for saying "no."

Endnotes

1 Stephen Colbert, "The Word—Disintegration," *The Colbert Report*, episode 07010, January 18, 2011.

2 Gerald Grant, *Hope and Despair in the American City: Why There Are No Bad Schools in Raleigh* (Harvard University Press, 2009), 2.

3 Ibid., 3.

4   Ibid., 8-9.

5   Ibid., 39.

6   Ibid., 66.

7   Gary Orfield, *Reviving the Goal of an Integrated Society: A 21st Century Challenge* (Los Angeles: UCLA Civil Rights Project, 2009).

8   James S. Coleman et al., *Equality of Educational Opportunity* (Washington, D.C.: National Center for Education Statistics, 1966).

9   Ibid., 22.

10 Richard D. Kahlenberg, *All Together Now: Creating Middle-Class Schools through Public School Choice* (Washington, D.C.: Brookings Institution, 2001), 25.

11 Heather Schwartz, *Housing Policy Is School Policy: Economically Integrative Housing Promotes Academic Success in Montgomery County, Maryland* (New York: Century Foundation, 2010).

12 Caroline Hoxby, *Peer Effects in the Classroom: Learning From Gender and Race Variation* (Cambridge, MA: National Bureau of Economic Research, 2000).

13 Eric A. Hanushek, John F. Kain, and Steven G. Rivkin, "New Evidence about *Brown v. Board of Education*: The Complex Effects of School Racial Composition on Achievement," *Journal of Labor Economics* 27, no. 3 (2009): 349–83.

14 Scott Imberman, Adriana D. Kugler, and Bruce Sacerdote, *Katrina's Children: Evidence on the Structure of Peer Effects from Hurricane Evacuees* (Cambridge, MA: National Bureau of Economic Research, 2009).

15 Kahlenberg, *All Together Now*, 48–49.

16 Ibid., 52.

17 Barack Obama, "Prepared Remarks of President Barack Obama: Back to School Event," Arlington, VA, September 8, 2009.

18 Kahlenberg, *All Together Now*, 54.

19 Ibid., 61-67.

20 See the Education Trust's webpage "Funding Fairness" at http://www.edtrust.org/issues/pre-k-12/funding-fairness.

21 Marguerite Roza, "How Districts Shortchange Low-Income and Minority Students," in *Funding Gaps* (Washington, D.C.: Education Trust, 2006), 9–12.

22 Eric A. Hanushek, "Valuing Teachers," *Education Next* 11, no. 3 (2011): 40–45.

23 However, brand-new research that looks at how much "value" a teacher adds in terms of students' progress on test scores indicates that effective teachers can be found in rich *and* poor schools. Likewise, ineffective teachers are found in all schools, too. Needless to say, the true distribution of teachers is a matter of great debate.

24 C. Kirabo Jackson, *School Competition and Teacher Labor Markets: Evidence from Char-*

ter School Entry in North Carolina (Cambridge, MA: National Bureau of Economic Research, 2011).

25   Douglas N. Harris, "High Flying Schools, Student Disadvantage, and the Logic of NCLB," *American Journal of Education* 113, no. 3 (2007): 367–94.

26   Jane L. David, Katrina Woodworth, Elizabeth Grant, Roneeta Guha, Alejandra Lopez-Torkos, and Viki M. Young, *Bay Area KIPP Schools: A Study of Early Implementation First Year Report 2004–05* (Menlo Park, CA: SRI International, 2006).

27   Amy Stuart Wells, Jacquelyn Duran, and Terrenda White, "Refusing to Leave Desegregation Behind: From Graduates of Racially Diverse Schools to the Supreme Court," *Teachers College Record* 110, no. 12 (2008): 2532–70.

28   Rhiana Maidenberg, "Sending My Kids to Public School: Why Being a Part of the System Is How to Fix It," *Babble*, March 6, 2012, http://www.babble.com/kid/kids-school-learning/choosing-public-school/.

29   Peter B. Wood and Nancy Sonleitner, "The Effect of Childhood Interracial Contact on Adult Antiblack Prejudice," *International Journal of Intercultural Relations* 20, no. 1 (1996): 1–17; and Tamara Towles-Schwen and Russel H. Fazio, "On the Origins of Racial Attitudes: Correlates of Childhood Experiences," *Personality and Social Psychology Bulletin* 27 (2001): 162–75.

2

Diversity's Downside:
Exploring the Risks

In 1985, I was a shy sixth grader at Claymont Elementary School in the Parkway School District in West St. Louis County, Missouri. My family lived in a typical Midwestern development called Meadowbrook Farms, which before the mid-1970s, when hundreds of ranch-style and faux-colonial houses sprouted from its fields, probably *was* a farm. My parents paid $60,000 for our house, and my father commuted twenty minutes to his job at his company's suburban corporate headquarters. Maybe once a month, we'd venture the twenty-five miles into St. Louis to see a Cardinals baseball game, visit the zoo, or watch a show. But these were just commando trips: get in, attend the sporting or cultural event, and get out. St. Louis was not a spot where we wanted to linger.

West County was known as a "nice place to grow up." It was relentlessly boring, with seemingly little history or sense of place, but it was certainly safe. As middle schoolers we went to Queeny Park on Friday nights to ice skate, and to the teen dance party at a local Lutheran church on Saturdays. A wild night out involved a trip to the arcade that was attached to the multiplex movie theater. It was *Leave it to Beaver*, 1980s-style.

Like the Cleavers' town of Mayfield, West County was unabashedly white. From Kindergarten through fifth grade, I don't recall having had a single black classmate, and I don't think I had ever even *seen* anyone who was Hispanic.

Were it not for *The Cosby Show* and Michael Jackson, my classmates and I wouldn't have known a single thing about black culture.

So you can only imagine what it must have been like to be Brian Harvey. Brian was the very first "transfer student" to make his way into Claymont's sixth grade. He was black. He was tall. And he was a sensation. I'll never forget Brian break-dancing in the middle of a circle of us puny, parachute-pants-wearing white kids, who were cheering and clapping furiously. It might not have been *exactly* what Martin Luther King, Jr., had in mind, but it was definitely something.

■ ■ ■

In 1983, St. Louis and its suburbs embarked on the largest, most expensive, and most ambitious desegregation plan in American history. Its primary intent was to address the stark segregation of St. Louis's black students, a significant portion of whom attended all-black schools in 1980—twenty-five years after *Brown*. Under threat of a lawsuit and the possibility of a forced merger with the city schools, more than a dozen suburban districts agreed as part of the plan to accept transfer students. The court required the state to pay the busing expenses, as well as the per-pupil cost of educating students from the city. By the mid-1990s, almost 15,000 black students were riding school buses from St. Louis to suburban districts every day.[1]

Parkway—one of the most affluent, high-performing systems in the state—was one of those districts. Brian was the first of a trickle of city students to reach our suburb. A few years later, by the time I was in high school, black kids made up about 20 percent of our freshman class.

By all accounts, they thrived in the program. A study by Robert Lissitz, from the University of Maryland, showed that the black transfer students in St. Louis's program made more progress in reading and math, particularly at the high school level, than their peers who stayed behind in city schools.[2] They also graduated at higher rates and were more likely to attend college.[3] Granted, the students who signed up for long bus rides likely were more motivated to learn than students who didn't, and their parents probably put a greater focus on education. Plus, receiving districts could screen out students with discipline problems. Still, the transfer students probably did better than they would have without the desegregation program.

Nor were there any signs that the white suburban students did worse academically because of the program. But how could we have? After that sixth-grade experience with Brian, I almost never saw another transfer student in class. In middle school I was tracked into advanced courses, and I stayed in that track through honors and Advanced Placement courses in high school. The transfer kids—having spent their formative years in low-performing elementary schools—were hopelessly behind, and most toiled in remedial reading and math.

Our classrooms were not really desegregated. In many ways, our high school as a whole still wasn't either. The cafeteria looked like a white sea with a small black island in the middle. Pep rallies and school assemblies were much the same. Black and white students were under the same roof, but we were hardly learning together in any meaningful sense.

We weren't completely separated. Sports teams provided the best opportunities for true integration, and sure enough, I made some black friends on the track-and-field team. Student council was another such opportunity: A few brave transfer students got themselves elected and participated as much as they could. (It wasn't easy; afternoon activity buses were sparse, and more than a few times the school picked up the tab for taxis to take city students home when they stayed late.)

Perhaps the most remarkable thing about the experience for me is how it didn't seem like a very big deal at the time. What I didn't realize was that the program was hugely controversial—"the whipping boy of Missouri politics," as William Freivogel, formerly a reporter at the *St. Louis Post-Dispatch*, put it to me. It played a big role in the election of John Ashcroft as Missouri governor in 1984 (he was dead-set against the program, as were many who voted for him) and remained contentious into the 1990s.

What drove these politics—beyond outright racism—was fear. White parents understandably wanted to protect their children from the mean streets of St. Louis, which was then in the midst of the crack cocaine epidemic, and didn't necessarily welcome this unexpected intrusion into their suburban tranquility. And their fears weren't entirely groundless, as I can attest. I was a junior, cruising through the empty hallways of our school, heading to perform some student council errand during the middle of third period, when a black transfer student walked by, reached out, yanked a gold chain off of my neck, and ran. After a few moments of stunned silence and then a fruitless attempt to chase him down, I found an assistant principal and told him what happened. Within minutes the culprit had been caught gold-handed, and within the hour I was called into the principal's office to I.D. him.

The student was given a sixty-day suspension. I felt pretty shaken up by the incident, but my primary emotion was guilt. I knew that kid was never coming back to Parkway West High School, and that I'd just played a role in a turning point in his life that was not for the best. It was the first time that I really thought about what it might be like to grow up outside of West County. I was starting to develop a social consciousness.

So, as Freivogel said to me, the desegregation program wasn't "some totally ideal Camelot." Our schools were never really integrated in the truest sense, and there were isolated incidents of violence and racial tension. Still, Freivogel said, "It was better than having all-white schools and all-black schools." Indeed.

Will a Diverse School Slow Down My Child?

Are diverse schools safe? How do they handle the inevitable racial and class tensions that ensue? Are they academically challenging? How do they manage the academic diversity of their students?

If you're a parent with small children, you want to find a school where they can thrive. You want them to be happy, safe, and well-adjusted, but also challenged and excited to learn. And ten or fifteen years down the road, you want them to be well-positioned to go to a good college and enjoy all of the opportunities that such an experience provides.

Regardless of how progressive you consider yourself to be, you don't want to jeopardize your child's future. Would our kids learn more if surrounded by children from other well-educated, middle-class families? Is that why so many wealthy families pay big bucks for private schools or move to exclusive suburbs? Is sending our kids to schools with poor kids a big gamble?

Here's the good news: Regardless of which schools your children attend, they are very likely to do well academically and go to college. Recall the famous Coleman study: The most important driver of academic achievement wasn't a child's school or teachers or textbooks or classmates. It was the child's parent. If you are well-educated, your child is highly likely to do well in school.

That's because of what you are already doing as your children's first teacher: showing an interest in their learning, reading to them, checking their homework, providing a safe and supportive environment at home, enriching their education with trips to museums and libraries and historical sites, and expecting them to go to college.

But that doesn't mean that school quality and composition are irrelevant. We already established that peer effects can have a big impact on poor and minority students; they are clearly better off with a critical mass of wealthier, higher-achieving peers. But what about your kids? Would they be dragged down by lower-achieving classmates?

The encouraging news is that middle-class students generally do fine in diverse settings, with a couple of important caveats. The first research to look at this question sprang from desegregation programs of decades ago. Without exception, these studies found white students were unharmed by the initiatives, just as my classmates and I were in St. Louis. David Armor, a professor emeritus in public policy at George Mason University and an opponent of busing, admitted more than a decade ago that "virtually all studies of desegregation and achievement have found little or no change in achievement or other educational outcomes for white children."[4]

And as we explored in Chapter One, scholars have looked at this question in more rigorous ways since then. While researchers such as Hoxby and Hanushek found that all students generally performed better when their peers were more affluent and higher-achieving, and worse when their peers were poorer and lower-achieving, the significance for white and middle-class students was negligible. Remember Hoxby's study of Texas students? Increasing a cohort's proportion of black students by ten percentage points lowered black achievement gains quite significantly, but just barely decreased white gains. That's not nothing—but it's also not reason to scratch diverse schools off your list completely.

All Together Now?

One reason diverse schools are not risk free is that such schools are much more likely to serve disruptive students. And those students *can* slow down your child's progress. That's the upshot of another recent peer effects study, a heart-wrenching one by economists Scott Carrell and Mark Hoekstra. They dug into domestic abuse data from the Alachua County Courthouse in Florida, and linked those files with student records from the county's school district. Almost 5 percent of Alachua County students had been exposed to some sort of domestic violence. Those students tended to perform much worse academically than their peers, and got into trouble more often too. But here's the kicker: Having those students as peers also reduced the academic performance of the other kids in the class. This effect was particularly strong for the highest-income students, especially, for some reason, white boys.[5]

The point isn't so much about domestic abuse, it's about disruptive students, who can negatively impact the performance of their peers—and who are more likely to come from poor families than from middle-class ones.[6]

There's another risk involved in sending middle-class children to diverse schools. In order for them to thrive there, Richard Kahlenberg argues, students need to be put in classrooms or small groups with other kids who are performing at about the same level, as I was at Parkway West. It's easy to understand why schools might do performance grouping, as it's called. "It is difficult for one math teacher to instruct a class that simultaneously includes gifted children who can handle advanced math and slower students who have not yet mastered the multiplication tables," Kahlenberg wrote. "Slower students are likely to feel swamped and frustrated, and faster students bored and unchallenged, by a pacing aimed at the middle of the class."[7]

This is true for all public schools that serve students coming in with a wide range of skills and abilities. But because of stark differences in family backgrounds, opportunities, and resources, the range of academic abilities tends to be larger in socioeconomically and racially mixed schools. (On average, middle-class children are two to three grade levels ahead of their low-income peers at any given time.[8]) And that makes it that much harder for teachers to instruct all students together.

Mind you, the use of performance grouping or tracking—whereby students are placed in semi-permanent tracks, such as "honors" or "on-level"—is controversial. Many educators and scholars argue that separating students by performance is just another form of segregation, particularly when the groups break down largely by race or class. And it's certainly true that some white middle-class parents push to get their students into "gifted" programs as a way to isolate them from poor or minority children. (In the 1990s in Alexandria, Virginia—a close-in suburb of Washington, D.C., where the majority of public school students are African American or Hispanic— virtually *all* of the white elementary school students were enrolled in the gifted and talented program.[9]) It's also true that for decades, many high-potential poor and minority kids were pushed into lower tracks when they could have succeeded in challenging college-preparatory courses. As a result of these concerns, and of images of all-white honors courses and all-black remedial classes, there was a major push in the '90s to "detrack" schools and teach all students together in heterogeneous classrooms.

But research shows that while teaching students of mixed ability together in one classroom is generally helpful for the low achievers, it's harmful for the high achievers. In 1995, scholars Dominic Brewer, Daniel Rees, and Laura Argys analyzed test score results for high school students in tracked and detracked classrooms, and found benefits of tracking for advanced students. They wrote, "The conventional wisdom on which detracking policy is often based—that students in low-track classes (who are drawn disproportionately from poor families and from minority groups) are hurt by tracking while others are largely unaffected—is simply not supported by very strong evidence."[10]

Tracking critics tend to dispute these findings, or at least argue that it doesn't have to be this way, that excellent teachers can "differentiate" their instruction to reach high and low achievers at the same time. As Gary Orfield told me, "If the teacher knows what to do, she can handle a lot of diversity."

The notion behind differentiated instruction is that one teacher instructs a diverse group of kids and manages to reach each one at precisely the appropriate level. The idea, according to Carol Tomlinson of the University of Virginia, is to "shake up what goes on in the classroom so that students have multiple options for taking in information, making sense of ideas, and expressing what they learn."[11] Ideally, instruction is customized at the individual-student level. Every child receives a tailored curriculum that meets his or her exact needs. A teacher might give specialized homework assignments, for example, or provide the specific one-on-one help that a particular kid requires.

If you think that sounds hard to do, you're not alone. I asked Holly Hertberg-Davis, who studied under Tomlinson and is now her colleague at Virginia, if differentiated instruction was too good to be true. Some teachers can pull it off, she said—but not all.

Hertberg-Davis worked with Tomlinson on a large study of differentiated instruction. Teachers were provided with extensive professional development and ongoing coaching. Three years later the researchers wanted to know if the program had had an impact on student learning. But they were stumped. "We couldn't answer the question," Hertberg-Davis told me, "because no one was actually differentiating."

Teachers admit to being flummoxed. In a 2008 national survey, more than eight in ten teachers said that differentiated instruction was "very" or "somewhat" difficult to implement.[12] Likewise, in a 2010 survey, that same share of education school professors also said differentiation was hard to implement.[13] (Both surveys were published by the Thomas B. Fordham Institute.)

Which brings us back to performance grouping. The more recent peer effects research (explored in Chapter One) shows the benefits of grouping students of similar abilities together. Think back to the Katrina study, for example. The arrival of low-achieving New Orleans students dragged down the scores of both low-performing and high-performing Houston students, but the effect was more pronounced for the high achievers. As one of the study's authors, Bruce Sacerdote, told me, "The high-achieving kids seemed to be the most sensitive. They do particularly well by having high-achieving peers. And they are particularly harmed by low-achieving peers." He added, "I've become a believer in tracking."

In 2006, Caroline Hoxby and Gretchen Weingarth examined the Wake County Public Schools in and around Raleigh, North Carolina. For the better part of two decades, the district had been reassigning lots of students to new schools every year in order to keep its schools racially and socioeconomically balanced. That created thousands of natural experiments whereby the composition of classrooms changed dramatically, and randomly. That, in turn, provided Hoxby and Weingarth an opportunity to investigate the impact of these changes on student achievement.

They found evidence for what they called the "Boutique model" of peer effects, "in which students do best when the environment is made to cater to their type."[14] When school reassignments resulted in the arrival of students with either very low or very high achievement, this boosted the test scores of other students who were on par academically with the newcomers. This result probably occurs because the assignments created a critical mass of students at the same achievement level, and schools could better focus attention on that group's particular needs.

Does that mean students should be sharply sequestered by performance? Not exactly. Here's how Hoxby and Weingarth put it:

> Our evidence does not suggest that complete segregation of people, by types, is optimal. This is because (a) people do appear to benefit from interacting with peers of a higher type and (b) people who are themselves high types appear to receive sufficient benefit from interacting with peers a bit below them that there is little reason to isolate them completely. What our evidence *does* suggest is that efforts to create interactions between lower and higher types ought to maintain continuity of types.[15]

What that means for classrooms is that it's okay for there to be a range of students (say high, medium, and low achievers), as long as that range is not too wide. What's pernicious is when there is a "bimodal" distribution of students in the same class: just very high achievers and very low achievers, with few pupils in between. It's not hard to understand why: How on earth could a teacher instruct such a group of students effectively?

Yet in the heyday of desegregation and busing, many programs mixed extremely high-achieving white students with extremely low-achieving black students. Tom Kane, a Harvard professor and one-time advisor to the Bill & Melinda Gates Foundation, brought this to my attention. He and his colleagues conducted a study in Charlotte, NC, a district that was nearly half black, after its busing program ended. They pored over test score data for the last few years of busing and noticed an unusual pattern: The wealthiest schools in the most affluent suburbs had fewer students passing state tests than you would expect. These schools should have been the highest-achieving ones, but they weren't.

It finally dawned on Kane what was happening: These schools had been desegregated by the poorest, lowest-achieving black students in the district—and many of those black students weren't passing the state tests, bringing down the schools' averages, even while the white students' scores remained high. This wasn't by design; it was an unintended consequence of transportation logistics.

Imagine, Kane said, a school in a neighborhood that's just 2 percent black, which must be reassigned to be 30 percent black. The transportation planner is not going to send ten buses into neighborhoods that are one-third black. Instead, he's going to think about efficiency, and send two buses into a neighborhood that's all black. The problem is, the all-black neighborhoods tended also to be the poorest ones. So these busing plans mixed the highest-income white kids not with average-performing black students, but rather with the neediest ones.

If this analysis is true, it presents a puzzle: How could well-off white students, who were likely to be extremely high-achieving, not be hurt by the arrival of low-income black students, who were likely to be extremely low-achieving? How is it that studies of desegregation found again and again that white students were unharmed, when Hoxby's study seems to indicate that schools with a bimodal distribution of students—with kids at just the top and the bottom—are bad for everyone?

The answer is simple: Desegregation led to integrated schools, but not integrated classrooms. As happened at my alma mater outside St. Louis, students were grouped by performance, so they could benefit from "boutique" instruction. White students couldn't be slowed down by lower-achieving black students, because those students weren't in their classes.

Desegregated Schools, Segregated Classrooms

Welcome to our first dilemma-within-a-dilemma. Let's say you decide to send your child to a racially and socioeconomically diverse school—because you want to live in the city, because you want your child to grow up in a diverse setting, and because you want to help poor kids climb out of poverty. But if your child is high-achieving (and what parent *doesn't* think her child is high achieving?), you also want her to be challenged and engaged. You probably want her to be in a classroom with other high achievers. In general, however, those are going to be other affluent kids from well-educated families. So now you're contemplating sending your child into a segregated classroom in an integrated school. And what's the point of that?

As Kahlenberg admits, a real tension is at work here. Many of the benefits of integrated schools accrue to poor and minority students only if their classrooms are also integrated. (The peer effects studies by Caroline Hoxby and Eric Hanushek showed the negative impact of segregated *classrooms*, not schools, particularly for African American students.) Likewise, it's hard for your kids to benefit from diversity if they spend most of their days in segregated classes.

But Kahlenberg still thinks school integration is worth it. "If you think about it," he said to me, "in [poor] schools that are economically segregated, essentially everyone is in the low track. You are tracking *by* school instead of *within* schools." Furthermore, he argued, at least some courses, like gym and music, aren't grouped by performance. Sports and other extracurricular activities provide opportunities for kids of different classes and races to get to know one another as well.

As we learned in Chapter One, those social contacts can be as important to poor children as any direct academic benefits they might glean from their higher-achieving, wealthier peers. And don't forget the political benefits of integrated schools. Savvy middle-class parents who know how to work the system can pressure school and district administrators to address problems, identify resources, and respond to concerns. That activism benefits everyone in a school, even kids attending segregated classes.

Still, the ideal situation for low-achieving kids is to be in class with higher-achieving peers most of the school day. But the ideal situation for high-achieving kids is to be with other high achievers most of the day. If there's a sure way to square that circle, I haven't been able to find it.

How About Safety?

Perhaps you're starting to get your head around the idea of sending your beloved children to a diverse school, but you've got one last nagging question: Will they be safe? You'd be crazy not to ask this question: Reams of research show safety to be high on the list of parent demands when shopping for schools.[16]

At first blush, the story for diverse schools is not a happy one. Take a look at figures 1, 2, and 3, drawn from federal school safety data for the 2007–08 school year.[17]

There's no getting around a basic fact: Affluent schools are safer than socioeconomically mixed schools, which are safer than high-poverty schools. That's not a big shock, but it's still sobering to see it in such sharp relief.

For me, figure 3 is particularly disturbing. Serious violent incidents include rape or attempted rape, other sexual battery, physical attack or fight with a weapon, threat of physical attack with a weapon, and robbery with or without a weapon. Economically integrated schools experience 73 percent more such incidents than predominantly affluent schools do; for high-poverty schools,

Figure 1. Crime Incidents per 100,000 Students, by Low-Income Enrollment

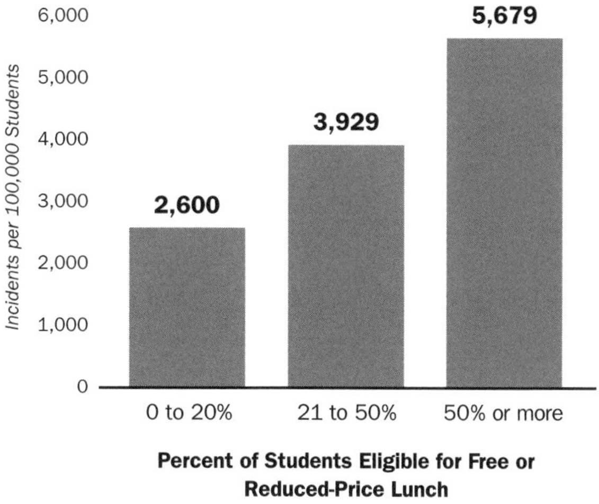

Incidents per 100,000 Students

- 2,600 — 0 to 20%
- 3,929 — 21 to 50%
- 5,679 — 50% or more

Percent of Students Eligible for Free or Reduced-Price Lunch

Source: National Center for Education Statistics, *Digest of Education Statistics 2010* (Washington, D.C.: National Center for Education Statistics, May 2011), table 168.

it's almost 300 percent more. We can't be expected to take such a huge risk with our kids, can we?

Well, not so fast. Yes, affluent schools are safer than diverse schools. But these are differences at the margins; your children are still highly unlikely to experience violence, regardless of the school they attend, because the frequency of violent incidents remains small in all schools. In general, schools are much safer than our society at large.

Consider this: In 2009, the violent crime rate in the United States was at its lowest point in history, with about 1,700 crimes per 100,000 people.[18] (Violent crimes include rape, robbery, assault, and homicide.) Compare that to a rate of serious violent crimes (a more inclusive definition) of 88 per 100,000 students at economically integrated schools. Americans in general are almost twenty times more likely to be victims of a violent crime than are students while they are at their diverse schools.

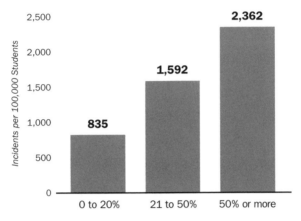

**Figure 2. Physical Fights or Attacks
without a Weapon per 100,000 Students,
by Low-Income Enrollment**

Source: National Center for Education Statistics, *Digest of Education Statistics 2010* (Washington, D.C.: National Center for Education Statistics, May 2011), table 168.

And violence isn't the only risk parents worry their children will encounter at school. Take a look at figure 4.

Based on these data, risk-adverse parents should consider high-poverty schools for their children, because they don't have much of a drug problem.

No Perfect Solutions

Are you more conflicted than ever before about where to send your child to school?

On the one hand, if what you value above all else is maximizing your child's academic potential, there's a strong argument for finding a school full of high-achieving students. The easiest way to do that is to move to the most affluent suburb you can afford, or move to a college town, or enroll your child in an exclusive private school. (Public "exam schools," where students have to qualify for admission, may be another option.) These are well-trodden

Figure 3. Serious Incidents per 100,000 Students, by Low-Income Enrollment

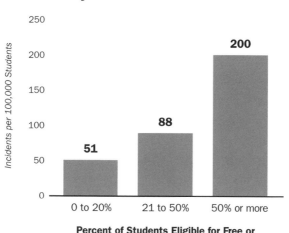

Source: National Center for Education Statistics, *Digest of Education Statistics 2010* (Washington, D.C.: National Center for Education Statistics, May 2011), table 168.

Note: "Serious incidents" include rape or attempted rape, other sexual battery, physical attack or fight with a weapon, threat of physical attack with a weapon, and robbery with or without a weapon.

paths, but they mean abandoning the idea that your child will experience socioeconomic diversity in school. (You can, of course, find other ways to introduce your child to kids from other cultures, such as through sports teams or at church.)

On the other hand, if you do send your child to an economically and racially diverse school, you are taking some (very small) risks with their safety and some (more significant) risks with their academic learning, particularly if that school doesn't group students by performance and your child is high-achieving. Yet an integrated school with segregated classrooms probably isn't what you were dreaming about when you started this journey.

Throw cultural differences into the mix, and this really gets tricky.

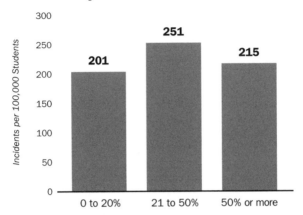

Figure 4. Distribution, Possession, or Use of Illegal Drugs per 100,000 Students, by Low-Income Enrollment

Source: National Center for Education Statistics, *Digest of Education Statistics 2010* (Washington, D.C.: National Center for Education Statistics, May 2011), table 168.

Endnotes

1   William H. Freivogel, "St. Louis: Desegregation and School Choice," in *Divided We Fail*, ed. Richard Kahlenberg (New York: Century Foundation, 2002), 209–35.

2   Robert W. Lissitz, *Assessment of Student Performance and Attitude Year IV—1994* (report to the Voluntary Interdistrict Coordinating Council), St. Louis, MO, December 1994. Cited by Freivogel, "St. Louis," 219.

3   Civic Progress Task Force, *Desegregation* (report from the Civic Progress Task Force on Desegregation of the St. Louis Public School System), December 1995; and Voluntary Interdistrict Coordinating Council for the Settlement Agreement, *Fourteenth Report to the United States District Court*, 1998. Both cited in Freivogel, "St. Louis," 220–21.

4   David J. Armor, *Forced Justice: School Desegregation and the Law* (New York: Oxford University Press, 1996), quoted in Richard D. Kahlenberg, *All Together Now: Creating Middle-Class Schools through Public School Choice* (Washington, D.C.: Brookings Institution, 2001), 39.

5   Scott E. Carrell and Mark L. Hoekstra, "Domino Effect," *Education Next* 9, no. 3 (2009): 59–63.

6   Kenneth A. Dodge, Gregory S. Pettit, and John E. Bates, "Socialization Mediators of

the Relation between Socioeconomic Status and Child Conduct Problems," *Child Development* 65 (1994): 649–65; and David T. Takeuchi, David R. Williams, and Russell K. Adair, "Economic Stress in the Family and Children's Emotional and Behavioral Problems," *Journal of Marriage and Family* 53, no. 4 (1991): 1031–41.

7   Kahlenberg, *All Together Now*, 136.

8   Math and reading scale scores from 2009 and 2011 are from National Center for Education Statistics NAEP Data Explorer, http://nces.ed.gov/nationsreportcard/naepdata/ (retrieved April 27, 2012).

9   Anecdotal evidence provided to the author by Dan Goldhaber, former member of the Alexandria City Board of Education.

10   Dominic J. Brewer, Daniel I. Rees, and Laura M. Argys, "Detracking America's Schools: The Reform without Cost?" *Phi Delta Kappan* 77, no. 3 (1995): 210–12, 214–15.

11   Carol Ann Tomlinson, *How to Differentiate Instruction in Mixed-Ability Classrooms*, 2nd ed. (Alexandria, VA: Association for Supervision & Curriculum Development, January 2001).

12   Steve Farkas, Ann Duffett, and Tom Loveless, *High-Achieving Students in the Era of No Child Left Behind* (Washington, D.C.: Thomas B. Fordham Institute, June 2008).

13   Steve Farkas and Ann Duffett, *Cracks in the Ivory Tower? The Views of Education Professors Circa 2010* (Washington, D.C.: FDR Group and Thomas B. Fordham Institute, September 2010).

14   Caroline M. Hoxby and Gretchen Weingarth, "Taking Race out of the Equation: School Reassignment and the Structure of Peer Effects" (working paper, Harvard University John F. Kennedy School of Government, Cambridge, MA, 2006,) 6.

15   Ibid., 30.

16   See, for example, Patrick J. Wolf and Thomas Stewart, "The Evolution of Parental School Choice," in *Customized Schooling: Beyond Whole-School Reform,* ed. Frederick Hess and Bruno Manno (Cambridge, MA: Harvard Education Press, 2011), 91-106.

17   National Center for Education Statistics, *Digest of Education Statistics 2010* (Washington, D.C.: National Center for Education Statistics, May 2011), table 168.

18   Office of Justice Programs, *National Crime Victimization Survey Violent Crime Trends, 1973–2008* (Washington, D.C.: Bureau of Justice Statistics, 2012).

3

Cultural Conflict in the Classroom

If you're tempted to plunge into a diverse school, it might be because you value the concept of a "common school," where rich and poor and black and brown and white all come together to learn under one roof. This ideal is a bedrock of the American story.

But is it realistic? Can one school be all things to all people?

Naomi Calvo is a recently minted Harvard Ph.D. who immersed herself in Seattle's "controlled choice" program for her dissertation. The intent of that effort, which offered parents public school options from across the city, was to better integrate Seattle's sharply segregated schools. The program required all parents to list their school preferences. Calvo later pored over these choices to look for patterns. How important was the proximity of the school to home? Test scores? Demographics? Did these preferences vary by race and class?

Calvo interviewed parents about their decision-making processes. One vignette is particularly telling:

> One morning I interviewed Sylvie, a vivacious middle class white mother whose daughter attended a popular alternative school. Sylvie was thrilled with the school—it was a perfect fit for her shy daughter, a nurturing close-knit community with project-based learning and a "child-centric" curriculum. The principal knew every student, and kids called teachers by their first names. The one downside, Sylvie said, was that the school was not as diverse as she would like. For some reason it had trouble attracting students of color, particularly black students.

Later that afternoon I interviewed Bernice, a middle class black mom who had chosen a large traditional school for her "social butterfly" daughter. Although the school had low test scores and a mediocre reputation, Bernice had been impressed when she visited. She thought the principal was pushing kids to excel, and liked the "collegebound" program that encouraged students to start thinking about college early. She was also attracted by the curriculum, which focused on basic skills. As Bernice described the different schools she considered and the various factors she weighed in choosing among them, I noticed that she did not mention Sylvie's alternative school as an option. Had she, I asked, considered sending her daughter there? "Oh no," Bernice replied. "That school, it doesn't have any discipline or structure whatsoever. Do you know," she went on in a horrified voice, "they even let the kids call teachers by their first names!"[1]

Of course, we dare not generalize from this one story; not all affluent white parents want progressive, open-ended schools, and not all black parents want highly structured, traditional ones. But there is some truth to this stereotype. It's hardly a secret: For decades, magnet school administrators have been placing Montessori schools in black neighborhoods as a way to draw white families, and "back-to-basics" schools in white neighborhoods to draw black families. And it works.

In the early 1990s, another Harvard graduate student, Maureen Allenberg Petronio, studied the public school choice program in Cambridge, Massachusetts. She found that parents tended to be either traditionalists, who wanted their kids to learn basic skills and get the "right answers," or alternative-school aficionadas, who sought environments that "stimulated curiosity and encouraged exploration," as she put it. Guess what? The alternative school parents were generally white professionals, while the traditionalists came from poorer backgrounds.[2]

More recent studies have confirmed these differences in parents' educational values. Economists Lars Lefgren and Brian Jacob looked at data from an unnamed school district regarding parents' requests for particular teachers. (About one in five parents made such requests every year.) What they found was that parents in more affluent schools placed a higher priority on teachers who created an enjoyable classroom environment, while parents in poor schools focused more on teachers who could raise student achievement.

It shouldn't come as any surprise that individuals from different cultures and backgrounds might have different values and preferences when it comes to their children's education. What may surprise you, however, is that it's not just a matter of preferences. Bernice, the black mom, was right to be alarmed by the alternative school and its lack of structure, because, as we'll learn, those types of schools have tended to be ineffective for minority kids. On the other hand, a highly structured school would have repelled Sylvie and may have bored her daughter. These moms haven't merely figured out what kind of school they would *like* for their daughters; they may have determined which type of school would educate them best.

So we've arrived at another dilemma-within-a-dilemma: It's hard to come up with a type of school that would appeal to both Bernice and Sylvie and serve both of their daughters well. Is it even possible for an integrated school to meet the needs of a diverse student body effectively, with such varied backgrounds, needs, and preferences?

Progressive Education: Good for "White Folks" Only?

In 1986, three years after receiving her Ed.D. from Harvard, Lisa Delpit published "Skills and Other Dilemmas of a Progressive Black Educator," an article that soon became one of the most requested in the *Harvard Educational Review*'s history. Delpit was born in Louisiana, where, as she put it, her teachers "in the pre-integration, poor black Catholic school that I attended corrected every other word I uttered in their effort to coerce my Black English into sometimes hypercorrect Standard English forms acceptable to black nuns in Catholic schools."[3]

But in her own teacher training and at Harvard, she learned from her professors that this "traditional" approach to education was shortsighted or even racist; that "people learn to write not by being taught 'skills' and grammar, but by 'writing in meaningful contexts.'" She took these theories and tried to implement them in an integrated school in Philadelphia. "The black kids went to school there because it was their only neighborhood school," she wrote ruefully. "The white kids went to school there because their parents had learned the same kinds of things I had learned about education. As a matter of fact, there was a waiting list of white children to get into the school. This was unique in Philadelphia—a predominantly black school with a waiting list of white children. There was no such waiting list of black children."[4]

While the older black teachers at the school focused on traditional skills such as handwriting and arranged their students' desks in parallel rows, Delpit embraced all of the progressive methods: open classrooms, learning stations, carpeted sitting areas instead of desks, math games, even weaving to teach fine motor skills.

"My white students zoomed ahead," Delpit wrote. "They worked hard at the learning stations. They did amazing things with books and writing. My black students played the games; they learned how to weave; and they threw the books around the learning stations. They practiced karate moves on the new carpets. Some of them even learned how to read, but none of them as quickly as my white students. I was doing the same thing for all my kids—what was the problem?"[5]

Delpit eventually adopted more traditional methods, which helped her black students improve their reading and writing skills. That's not to say that she rejected the tenets of progressive education entirely. But her article sparked an enormous response from other black teachers, who believed that the fashionable progressive methods were good for "white folks" but not for kids of color. And those teachers might have been right.

Enter Don Hirsch. In 1986, when Delpit published her article, Hirsch was a relatively low-profile English professor at the University of Virginia with such book titles to his credit as *Wordsworth and Schelling* and *Validity in Interpretation*. Like many of his colleagues in academe, his politics were leftish and his concerns for the poor sincere. But in 1987 he published *Cultural Literacy: What Every American Needs to Know*, and was immediately labeled a racist right-winger. What Hirsch argued was that all young people needed to possess "mainstream cultural knowledge" in order to navigate society's institutions and opportunities successfully. The research, he said, was clear: People who scored high on tests of cultural literacy did better educationally and economically. If America was serious about enabling social mobility, Hirsch argued, it had to ensure that all of its children had access to knowledge, which was the key to power.[6] But critics charged that he was merely trying to cement the "dead white male" canon and repress alternative cultural viewpoints.

In 1996, Hirsch expanded on *Cultural Literacy*'s arguments in *The Schools We Need and Why We Don't Have Them,* tracing the "thoughtworld" that dominates schools of education and has had such a strong impact on teachers-in-training nationwide. Like Delpit, Hirsch wasn't against progressive education per se. Hands-on, child-centered, active learning methods could all work fine in the hands of gifted teachers. Delpit's concern was the bias against teaching *skills*; Hirsch's was the antipathy toward imparting *knowledge*. Progressive educators regularly derided knowledge about history, literature, and science as "mere facts"; Hirsch saw the acquisition of such knowledge as the passport to opportunity in America.[7]

According to Hirsch, an "anti-knowledge" stance does great harm to the country's neediest students, who are the least likely to gain vital core knowledge outside of school. "There is not only a practical separation between educational conservatism and political conservatism, but something even stronger," he wrote in *The Schools We Need*. "There is an inverse relation between educational progressivism and social progressivism. Educational progressivism is a sure means for preserving the social status quo, whereas the best practices of educational conservatism are the only means whereby children from disadvantaged homes can secure the knowledge and skills that will enable them to improve their condition."[8]

And why is the acquisition of knowledge, versus "learning how to learn," so important to disadvantaged children? Hirsch offered this example: "When a teacher tells a class that electrons go around the nucleus of an atom as the planets go around the sun, that analogy might be helpful for students who already know about the solar system, but not for students who don't." In other words, he wrote, "relevant background knowledge can be conceived as a stock of potential analogies that enable new ideas to be assimilated."[9]

THE DIVERSE SCHOOLS DILEMMA

And for all of the reasons we explored in Chapters One and Two, middle-class kids are more likely than poor children to bring relevant background knowledge to school with them. Affluent kids have a huge head start because of their relatively large vocabularies, exposure to language through their parents' and peers' conversations, and enrichment activities (like trips to the zoo) that they've enjoyed practically since the womb. Many poor children, on the other hand, will build relevant background knowledge only if exposed to it in school. And if they don't build this knowledge in the early grades, they will fall even further behind as they get older.

Poor Kids, Promising Results

So if progressive education—at least the kind that downplays the teaching of knowledge—is not generally the best approach for the neediest kids, what is? What kinds of curriculum, pedagogy, and culture are seen in schools that teach disadvantaged children effectively?

One of the most compelling investigations of high-performing inner-city schools is David Whitman's *Sweating the Small Stuff: Inner-City Schools and the New Paternalism*. Whitman, a former *U.S. News* reporter who is now a speechwriter for Secretary of Education Arne Duncan, looked at six highly successful secondary schools—four charter schools, one Catholic school, and one regular public school. All are achieving phenomenal results as measured by test scores, graduation rates, and success in college, and all serve predominantly poor and minority students.

These schools are not cookie-cutter copies of one another; each has its own distinctive flavor. But, as Whitman reports, they share some key commonalities. "They all have rigorous academic standards, test students frequently, and carefully monitor students' academic performance to assess where students need help," he wrote.

None of this is surprising. Such traits have been identified by "effective schools" analysts for more than three decades. And these insights parallel what scientists have learned from forty years of study about how students best learn to read, much of it funded by the National Institutes of Health. Poor kids in particular need instruction that is direct and highly structured, and buttressed by regular assessment to determine whether the learning is sticking.

Whitman pointed out other staples of highly successful high-poverty schools: uniforms or a dress code, an extended school day, and summer school. But his unique contribution was to identify a secret ingredient in the schools' success that is often overlooked: They are all benignly *paternalistic*:

> Each of the six schools is a highly prescriptive institution that teaches students not just how to think but how to act according to what are commonly termed traditional, middle-class values . . . The schools tell students exactly how they are expected to behave and their behavior is closely monitored, with real rewards for compliance and penalties for noncompliance. Students are required to talk a certain way, sit a certain way, and dress a certain way.[10]

For example, Whitman wrote, at Amistad Academy in New Haven, Connecticut, teachers

> frequently tell students to 'correct their SLANT'—an acronym borrowed from KIPP that stands for Sit Up. Listen. Ask and answer questions. Nod your head so people know you are listening and understanding. Track the speaker by keeping your eyes on whoever is talking. At the end of class, students line up quietly, in the same order, and proceed to the next class or to the lunchroom.[11]

Here's another vignette, this one about the Cristo Rey Academy, a Jesuit school in Chicago that sends high school students to internships in professional office environments.

> The dress code . . . is remarkably detailed—and sure not to send teen hearts racing. Boys wear long-sleeved cotton or poplin shirts with collars and buttons and free of lettering and logos. Shirts must be buttoned all the way up and worn over plain white undershirts. A solid black or brown belt must be worn at all times. Trousers must have a crease and hem in the leg, and pants must be worn at the waistline. Leather or leather-like shoes in solid black or brown must hold a shine. A boy's hair cannot be long enough to cover his collar or longer than a #2 clipper attachment. Boys are shown, and practice, how to tie a tie. All the markings of teenhood and teen

rebellion—earrings, facial piercings, sun glasses, or corn rows—are flatly forbidden.

The dress code for girls is similarly drab: blouses buttoned all the way up, no white socks, no tight pants, no earrings larger than a quarter, and only soft colors used for eye shadow. Wearing a watch is recommended. But the watches cannot have sports logos or cartoon figures on the timepiece.[12]

Ready to enroll *your* kids?

There's no way my wife and I would send our sons to a "paternalistic" school. We'd be worried that the experience would be stultifying. We picture something much more warm and fuzzy, progressive, and creative.

Yet the evidence is clear that many poor students would flounder in such a laid-back environment, that they generally benefit from highly structured lessons, an initial focus on basic skills, the development of background knowledge, strict discipline, and careful cultivation of their habits, behavior, and aspirations.

Naomi Calvo put it to me bluntly: "The types of reforms that are considered best practice for disadvantaged kids are exactly what middle-class parents hate. I don't know how you are going to have a meeting of the minds on that." Partly this is about structure—affluent parents want the school day to end early enough so there's time for enrichment activities and sports practice, while poor kids need more learning time. But this is also about values. When asked about the attributes they want their children to develop in school, affluent parents tend to name "creativity" and "thinking outside the box." Poor parents, on the other hand, "don't use language like that," Calvo said. They speak in more concrete terms, and are focused on making sure their kids can read and do math and get ready for college.

A school can't be both paternalistic and loosey-goosey, both structured and open-ended. Students either call their teachers by their first names or they don't. Either they wear uniforms or they don't. It's hard for schools to meet the needs of poor kids while also meeting the expectations of affluent parents.

The Politics of Priorities: Whose Needs Count Most?

More than half of all parents in the United States now actively choose their kids' schools, either by enrolling their children in public schools outside of their communities (like a magnet or charter school), by going private, or by moving into particular neighborhoods in order to be zoned into preferred schools.[13] This expansion of choice means that schools don't have to be all things to all people anymore. They can adopt a particular academic focus and build a distinct culture, and then recruit teachers and parents who share similar values—educational and otherwise.

But not all schools enjoy this same luxury. Neighborhood "common schools" that must serve diverse groups with diverse needs and values have to navigate through the competing demands of their constituents to try to find compromises that keep everyone happy. This is far easier said than done, and sometimes school leaders have to set priorities and make tough choices. So who wins and who loses?

In the bad old days, it was easy to answer that question: Wealthy white kids won, and poor minority kids lost. Because affluent parents knew how to work the system and be the proverbial squeaky wheels, school boards and administrators learned to give them what they wanted to make the noise go away: the best teachers, the most challenging courses, and other critical resources. Poor kids, meanwhile, were left with rookie instructors and watered-down curricula.

The federal No Child Left Behind law set out to change all of that. By requiring schools to publish test scores for all groups of students (including minority students, low-income students, special education students, and so on), it made transparent the achievement gaps that had long existed in many schools but were hidden from view when folded into a single schoolwide average. And by threatening schools with penalties if they didn't get all groups of students up to standards, the law sought to force educators to shift their attention to the poor and minority kids who had always been "left behind." The law was redistributionist in nature: It sought to impact the internal politics of

Figure 5: Who Is Most Likely to Get One-on-One Attention from Teachers?

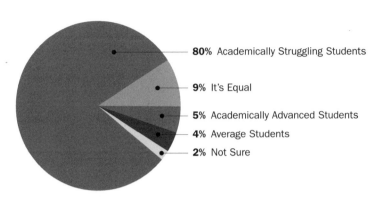

80% Academically Struggling Students

9% It's Equal

5% Academically Advanced Students

4% Average Students

2% Not Sure

Source: Steve Farkas, Ann Duffett, and Tom Loveless, *High-Achieving Students in the Era of No Child Left Behind* (Washington, D.C.: Thomas B. Fordham Institute, June 2008).

the 100,000 public schools nationwide by forcing them to make the education of disadvantaged and low-achieving children a priority.

On that score at least, it's been a big success. In one study, researchers Steve Farkas and Ann Duffett asked a nationally representative sample of teachers about how they allocated their scarcest resource: their time. Figure 5 shows what they said:[14]

There are reasons to be happy about this chart. "Academically struggling students" *should* be a high priority in our public schools; for too long their needs have been ignored and overlooked. If No Child Left Behind is pressuring educators to give these students their due, it's for the good.

As a parent, however—particularly if your child will likely be classified as "academically advanced"—you should go in with both eyes open. In schools that are predominantly white and affluent, teachers don't have to worry much about No Child Left Behind. Their students are going to pass the (almost uniformly) easy tests regardless of what happens in the classroom. These schools can set their sights on loftier targets: preparing students for Advanced Placement courses, getting kids into top-tier colleges, developing children's creativity.

But in diverse schools that serve lots of needy kids, teachers are under enormous pressure to get reading and math scores up to their states' yardstick of basic proficiency. Though this is changing in some places, getting them further than that has not really been rewarded so far. That can make high-achieving kids a low priority—and make the entire school less engaging and appealing by giving short shrift to subjects that don't count toward a school's status under NCLB, such as history, science, art, and music.

Amy Stuart Wells, the Columbia University professor, told me that if her kid attended a school at risk of missing the law's basic targets, she would worry that "the pedagogy would be very boring, because it would be about teaching to the test . . . Overall there is a lot of research to show that in schools that are struggling, the pedagogy stinks, it's boring, it's all drill-and-kill."

Consider this tale: E. L. Haynes Public Charter School is widely considered one of the highest-performing schools in Washington, D.C. It serves a student population that is two-thirds poor, yet it posts phenomenal gains on the District of Columbia's reading and math tests. It boasts incredibly talented and hardworking teachers, a crackerjack principal, and a high-powered board of directors. Many of the well-educated, upper-middle-class white parents in D.C. that I interviewed for this book dream of getting their kids into E. L. Haynes, even though their children would be minorities there.

Yet even this excellent school can't do it all. A friend of mine and his wife own a house in Washington's diverse Mount Pleasant neighborhood and love city living and their community. When their son became school-age, they placed his name into the lottery for E. L. Haynes.

Their son was picked for admission, and at first, all was well. My friend came to respect the school's principal and educators tremendously. He and his wife valued the diverse school community and E. L. Haynes's heroic efforts to involve the parents in meaningful ways. Their son liked the school too, and enjoyed making friends from across the city.

But before long it became clear that the school just wasn't going to work for their boy, who had tested several grade levels ahead in reading and math. Here's how my friend described the situation to me in an email:

[I]t's heavily focused on getting its kids to meet the DC-CAS [Comprehensive Assessment System] test, under the NCLB rules, and as a result a charter school that advertises itself as focused on "expeditionary learning" instead spends almost the entire year drilling kids for the test, then crams all its "expeditionary" content into the final few weeks of the year, after the tests, in the form of rapid-fire field trips . . . And of course the kids who are easily able to pass the DC-CAS are just left to hang out all year long. So at a fair amount of expense, both financial and lifestyle, we moved last week here to Maryland.

My friend is adamant that he isn't faulting E. L. Haynes. As he told me, "Haynes is doing a hell of a job bringing up kids from where they are to basic levels. And the school is showing up well on NCLB measures because that's what they are doing. But there are no NCLB measures for bringing kids higher than that bar."

Culture Clash

If you select a diverse school, you will be joining a diverse community, one that includes parents with different values regarding child rearing, education, and appropriate behavior. These parents, and their kids, will have an impact on your child's values and behavior. Are you ready for that?

There's little doubt that child-rearing practices tend to vary by social class. Compelling evidence on this front comes from Annette Lareau, the University of Pennsylvania sociologist quoted in the introduction. (You may also have read about her work in David Brooks's *New York Times* columns or in Malcolm Gladwell's *Outliers*.) She and her research colleagues devoted years to studying parenting practices up close and personal. They tracked twelve families of different racial and socioeconomic backgrounds, spending at least a month—often 24/7—embedded in their everyday routines. Whether in an SUV, on a front stoop, in the kitchen, or on a trip to the doctor, the researchers were there, watching everything that was happening.

They expected to find twelve different parenting styles—one per family. But in fact, they found just two, divided along class (not racial) lines:

Upper-middle-class parents practiced what Lareau called "concerted cultivation," and working-class and poor families practiced "natural growth."[15]

Concerted cultivation should strike a chord with you, though you've probably never labeled it as such. Middle-class parents they followed ensured that their children participated in a plethora of organized activities (sports, music lessons, and more) designed to help them develop their full range of talents. See if the following example from Lareau's book *Unequal Childhoods* sounds familiar:

> In the nineteenth century, families gathered around the hearth. Today, the center of the middle-class home is the calendar—the middle-class homes we visited typically had a large, white paper monthly calendar, hung on the wall above or next to the kitchen telephone. Scheduled, paid, and organized activities for children are noted (sometimes in a colored pen) in the two-inch-square open spaces beneath each day of the month. Month after month, children are busy participating in sports, music, scouts, and play groups. And, before and after going to work, their parents are busy getting them to and from these activities. At times, middle-class houses seem to be little more than holding places for the occupants during the brief periods when they are between activities.[16]

Parents also conversed with their kids frequently, encouraging them to share their feelings, speak up for what they want, reason, and negotiate. They engaged them in the kind of dialogue that makes children more effective communicators. Consider this conversation between a nine-year-old and his mother:

> As she drives, she asks Alex, "So, how was your day?" Alex: "Okay. We had hot dogs today, but they were burned! They were all black!" Christina: "Oh, great. You shouldn't have eaten any." Alex: "They weren't all black, only half were. The rest were regular." Christina: "Oh, okay. What was that game you were playing this morning?" Alex: "It was [called] 'Whatcha doin?'" Christina: "How do you play?"
>
> In this exchange, Ms. Williams is doing more than eliciting information from Alex. She is also giving him the opportunity to develop and practice verbal

skills, including how to summarize, highlight important details, clarify, and amplify information.[17]

Lareau argues that these practices, which many middle-class families do without thinking, are hugely beneficial for children in twenty-first-century America. They won't necessarily create happier children—the poor kids she studied generally seemed more relaxed than the affluent ones. But this kind of parenting will develop the skills, talents, and confidence that will help kids do well in school, college, and the white-collar world of work, where verbal agility and the ability to negotiate within institutions are a must.

The working-class and poor parents in Lareau's study, on the other hand, adopted a different philosophy. They believed in letting their kids be kids—to have plenty of unstructured time to play, to spend long summer days or weekends without supervision, and to make fun on their own. (Which, interestingly enough, is the polar opposite of the structure they want from their schools.) While they considered their children's safety to be their job, they don't feel the same about their development. Perhaps most importantly, they didn't tend to engage their children in much conversation—they issued orders and directives instead. This has its benefits—their kids tended to be more respectful to adults, less argumentative, and kinder to their siblings. But it has real costs in terms of preparing children for school and the workplace, as it results in fewer reasoning and negotiating skills, as well as the weaknesses in vocabulary and content knowledge that Don Hirsch blames for much of the academic divide.

Then there are the sharply different approaches to discipline. In many middle-class homes, children often debate, or even argue, with their parents, making their case for what they want. Parents, in general, reciprocate with reasoned counterarguments. The parties work toward an agreement that is acceptable to all involved. In poor households, on the other hand, the adults are more authoritarian—and use more physical punishment.

Because of the starkly different approaches to child rearing that Lareau identified (admittedly, with a very small sample), it's not crazy to think that that if our children attend socioeconomically diverse schools, they are more likely to encounter classmates who are being yelled at or ignored by or spanked by their parents. On the other hand, if we send them to predominantly upper-middle-class schools, we can be more optimistic that the majority of parents (though of course not all parents) share our basic values about how to raise children.

There's one more thing to consider. For all the happy talk about diversity, research shows that it can make people *more* isolated. Robert Putnam is a Harvard political scientist well known for his 2000 book *Bowling Alone,* which documented the collapse of civic organizations in America. More recently, he led a massive study of social engagement in different communities in the United States, and came to a deeply unsettling finding. People living in racially homogeneous communities, like those found in small towns in the Midwest, tended to be more politically active, more involved in civic organizations, and generally happier. On the other hand, individuals in diverse urban environments tended to act like turtles: They kept to themselves, volunteered less, and viewed the outside world with greater suspicion. In short, diverse communities developed less social capital than homogeneous ones.[18] Applied to education, this finding could imply that homogeneous schools also enjoy more social capital than diverse ones: greater participation at community events, stronger bonds among parents, easier relationships between staff and families, and so forth. In other words, diversity can be stressful.

But if my wife and I send our son to a homogeneous school, his life might be a lot like little Garrett Tallinger's, another one of Lareau's subjects:

> Garrett's friends are white, as are most of the people he interacts with, whether he is at home, at school, or on the playing field. The family's baby-sitters are white teenagers; the man who comes to mow the lawn is white as well. Among the children in the two fourth-grade classes at Garrett's school, there are three Blacks and one Asian; about 90 percent of the school's total enrollment is white. Garrett's piano teacher is white, and so are all the members of the piano recital crowd. His swim team is all white. In fact, the field-worker who accompanied the Tallingers to their country club (for swim practice) saw only white children, parents, and club staff out by the pool (except for one Black swim instructor). Garrett's all-white base-ball team occasionally plays teams that include Black children.[19]

Ugh.

The Dilemma Revisited

Are you curled up in the fetal position yet? What began as a simple question—"Should we send our kids to the diverse school down the street?"—turns out to be riddled with complexity, ambiguity, and angst. When my wife and I were trying to answer this question for our own sons, we turned to a trusty tool: the pro/con list.

The "pro" side has lots on it:

- Sending our sons to a diverse school would give them an opportunity to learn how to live in diverse twenty-first-century America.

- It would provide exciting and enriching multicultural opportunities they can't experience in a homogeneous school.

- It would reinforce our commitment to the "common school" ideal. We would be standing up to "separate but equal," and helping our sons' poor classmates learn more about the world than they would if segregated into schools with only other poor children.

- We'd get to stay in Takoma Park, which we love.

But the "con" side is persuasive, too:

- We would probably have to give up on finding anything too progressive or artsy or unstructured.

- We would be taking some (small) risks with our kids' safety, and would increase the odds that they'd have one or more disruptive students in class with them, which could slow them down academically.

- If we chose a school that grouped students by performance—which might be best for our kids—classrooms themselves would probably be largely segregated.

For us, it's a close call. But for most upper-middle-class parents, it's simple: They would move to affluent suburbs, or send their children to private schools, rather than take a chance on schools with lots of poor kids. And their kids will do fine in these homogeneous schools, on the whole. But because they have been denied diversity, they will miss out on real-world experiences that might have shaped them in important ways.

Parents who choose a school with socioeconomic diversity are making a commitment. They are agreeing to tackle a certain amount of hassle and challenge that they otherwise wouldn't encounter. They may need to step out of their own comfort zones to build relationships with parents from other races and socioeconomic groups. They may need to be extra-involved in their children's schools, through volunteering, fundraising, political activism, and vigilance, and supplement the school day with plenty of enrichment activities.

This is tough stuff, a major life decision. But if you're still open to taking the plunge, keep reading. It's time to get personal, and talk about the school down the street from *you*.

Endnotes

1   Naomi Calvo, "How Parents Choose Schools: A Mixed-Methods Study of Public School Choice in Seattle" (doctoral dissertation, Harvard University John F. Kennedy School of Government, 2007), 32.

2   Maureen Allenberg Petronio, "The Choices Parents Make," *Educational Leadership* 54 (1996): 33–36.

3   Lisa Delpit, "Skills and Other Dilemmas of a Progressive Black Educator," in *Other People's Children: Cultural Conflict in the Classroom* (New York: New Press, 1995), 11.

4   Ibid., 12-13.

5   Ibid., 13.

6   E. D. Hirsch, *Cultural Literacy: What Every American Needs to Know* (New York: Houghton Mifflin, 1987).

7   E. D. Hirsch, *The Schools We Need and Why We Don't Have Them* (New York: Doubleday, 1996).

8   Ibid., 7.

9   Ibid., 23.

10   David Whitman, *Sweating the Small Stuff: Inner-City Schools and the New Paternalism* (Washington, D.C.: Thomas B. Fordham Institute, June 2008), 3.

11   Ibid., 102.

12   Ibid., 130.

13   Sarah Grady, Stacey Bielick, and Susan Aud, *Trends in the Use of School Choice: 1993 to 2007* (Washington, D.C.: National Center for Education Statistics, 2010).

14   Steve Farkas, Ann Duffett, and Tom Loveless, *High-Achieving Students in the Era of No Child Left Behind* (Washington, D.C.: Thomas B. Fordham Institute, 2008).

15   Annette Lareau, *Unequal Childhoods: Class, Race and Family Life* (Berkeley, CA: University of California Press, 2003).

16   Ibid., 63–64.

17   Ibid., 116–17.

18   Robert D. Putnam, "*E Pluribus Unum:* Diversity and Community in the Twenty-First Century," *Scandinavian Political Studies* 30 (2007): 137–74.

19   Lareau, *Unequal Childhoods*, 42.

4

Finding the Right Diverse School for Your Child

Chances are, you're reading this book because you live in or near the city, want to stay, and are trying to decide whether the school around the corner will work for your child. This chapter will help you figure out whether it's a good fit. But it's also likely that you have some choices beyond your own neighborhood school. In almost every city in America today, parents can choose schools outside of their own communities—charter schools and magnet schools especially—so we'll discuss how to sort through those options, too.

In some locales, the number of choices can feel overwhelming. Washington, D.C., for example, boasts one hundred charter schools. Where to begin?

This barrage of choices isn't limited to school searches, of course. Anyone looking for a new home, for instance, faces a similar challenge. But the solution there is fairly straightforward. First, determine which criteria are most important to you, such as the price range, location, and number of bedrooms. Then, using a site like Redfin, filter homes by those criteria until you're down to a manageable number. Explore those homes online, and then go visit the ones that look most promising.

According to Bill Jackson, the process of finding the right school is much the same. You've probably never heard Jackson's name, but I bet you've visited his website. In fact, you might even be addicted to it: GreatSchools.org.

GreatSchools is the premier online destination for finding and comparing schools. (In fact, it gets about as much traffic as Redfin.) It's packed full of information—test scores, graduation rates, parent reviews, and more—on virtually every school in America. While it was designed with working-class and middle-class families in mind, it's become a magnet for well-educated upper-middle-class parents, especially moms. (Not surprisingly, this makes the site an advertising gold mine.)

Bill Jackson is your prototypical social entrepreneur. His wiry frame and jumpy movements made me think of a runner on caffeine. (We did meet at a Starbucks, to be fair.) His silver rectangular eyeglasses, messy hair, and casual attire had Bay Area written all over them. His latest effort, funded by titans such as the Bill & Melinda Gates Foundation, is to develop an online training program for lower- and middle-income parents, so they can learn the tricks of concerted cultivation that Annette Lareau wrote about.

What Jackson recommends for parents searching for the right school for their kids is to "screen, match, and explore." First you screen out schools that are out of the question—maybe because of location, demographics, test scores, or other factors. Then you look for a match in terms of certain programs or philosophies. You can do this on GreatSchools, by reading parent reviews and getting a feel for the school. Then, most importantly, go visit a school and "ask questions about the culture, standards, leadership," Jackson said. "You see it up close."

A Tipping Point?

It's time for me to screen, match, and explore the local schools in my community, Takoma Park. First, I have to set my screen regarding demographics. I have to decide what amount of diversity feels right to me.

We learned in Chapter Two that, according to most studies, desegregation efforts didn't slow down the performance of white or middle-class students. However, there *is* evidence that such students learn less when they attend high-poverty schools—those where more than 50 percent of the students are poor.[1] Fifty percent seems to be a tipping point beyond which all students (rich and poor, black and white) do worse.[2] And, as we've already discovered, there's similar evidence that high-poverty schools tend to be significantly less safe than mixed-income or low-poverty schools.

Richard Kahlenberg—the advocate for the socioeconomic integration of our schools—admits as much. "You want an environment where your child's classmates are going to encourage achievement, where there's not going to be a lot of disruption, and where there's not going to be a lot of kids moving in and out of the classroom because of mobility," he told me. "You want some of the other parents volunteering in the classroom, keeping their eyes on things and helping teachers. And you want there to be parents who know how to fix things in the school when things go awry. So you want a core of middle-class parents. It doesn't have to be everyone, but a core. And you want high-quality teachers teaching to high expectations. None of that is likely to be found in high-poverty schools."

There isn't anything magical, of course, about 50 percent. Some schools could have a larger proportion of poor students and still enjoy a middle-class culture. And some schools might have a smaller proportion of poor students yet feel like a high-poverty school.

But Kahlenberg was blunt with his advice for parents considering high-poverty schools for their children: "Avoid them."

Not that he has to make much of a case, particularly to white families. In the Washington, D.C., metropolitan area, for example, less than 3 percent of white public school students attend schools where poor students are the majority.[3] This parallels the findings of Duke professor Charlie Clotfelter. He dug up historical data in the South that demonstrated a white exodus away from public schools when they became 50 percent black.[4]

To be clear, I'm not saying that you should flee your neighborhood public school if it's majority poor. Some of these schools could turn out to be great, and those that are questionable might still be responsible choices, particularly if their demographics are shifting. More on that in Chapter Five.

But for my kids, I'm setting the screen to look at schools that are majority middle class. Our neighborhood school—Piney Branch Elementary—makes the cut, with a 33 percent poverty rate.

Going Deeper: Using Test Scores Wisely

The second screen should be test scores: Let's eliminate schools whose student performance is in the tank, right? This is where it gets really complicated, because average test scores can be highly misleading. Here's a tutorial on how to use them effectively.

For illustrative purposes, let's compare five elementary schools in and around Takoma Park (table 1). We'll use ratings from GreatSchools, which ranks schools on a scale of 1 to 10 (10 is best) based on passing rates on state reading and math tests. What you see here are the GreatSchools ratings for 2010–11, as well as the share of students at the school who come from low-income families and various racial groups.

My first reaction, I'll admit, is: Why aren't there any 9s or 10s on this list? And my second reaction is: My sons are going to Sligo Creek or Woodlin! But let's deconstruct the table a bit. As I mentioned before, these GreatSchools. org ratings are based on state reading and math scores. A school gets a 10 if its pass rate on the tests is near the 100th percentile—in other words, if a greater proportion of its students passes the test than in almost every school in the state. And so forth on down the number scale. So Pine Crest's 5 means the school is about average (or at the 50th percentile) in terms of its pass rate on the state tests.

Table 1. Takoma Park Schools, by Income and Race

School	GreatSchools Rating	Low-Income	White	Black	Hispanic	Asian
Sligo Creek Elementary	8	23%	49%	28%	16%	7%
Woodlin Elementary	8	23%	43%	35%	12%	9%
Piney Branch Elementary	6	33%	32%	46%	15%	7%
Pine Crest Elementary	5	46%	30%	29%	26%	15%
Cresthaven Elementary	5	64%	8%	39%	45%	7%

Source: GreatSchools.org.

Table 2. Takoma Park Schools, by White Passing Rate

School	White Pass Rate in Reading	White Pass Rate in Math	GreatSchools Rating	Percent Low-Income	Percent White
Sligo Creek Elementary	≥95%	≥95%	8	23%	49%
Woodlin Elementary	≥95%	≥95%	8	23%	43%
Piney Branch Elementary	≥95%	≥95%	6	33%	32%
Pine Crest Elementary	≥95%	≥95%	5	46%	30%
Cresthaven Elementary	N/A	N/A	5	64%	8%

Source: GreatSchools.org.

But do you notice something going on in this table? The greater the pro-portion of poor kids, the lower the GreatSchools rating. Woodlin and Sligo Creek each get an 8, but they also serve an overwhelmingly middle-class population. Cresthaven gets a 5, but more than half of its kids are poor. And we've already established that, in general, affluent kids score higher on reading and math tests than poor kids do.

Table 3. Takoma Park Schools, by White Advanced Rate

School	White Students at Advanced in Reading	White Students at Advanced in Math	GreatSchools Rating	Percent Low-Income	Percent White
Sligo Creek Elementary	66%	62%	8	23%	49%
Woodlin Elementary	59%	56%	8	23%	43%
Piney Branch Elementary	73%	76%	6	33%	32%
Pine Crest Elementary	65%	64%	5	46%	30%
Cresthaven Elementary	N/A	N/A	5	64%	8%

Source: GreatSchools.org.

In truth, these average pass rates don't tell you a lot about what's going on inside the school. We don't know if the GreatSchools rating is telling us how well the kids are being educated, or just how poor they are. We don't know if these schools are bringing kids just over the proficiency bar, or well above it. But that doesn't mean test scores aren't useful. If we can dig deeper—and break the scores out by race and class—we'll get a more accurate picture. Thanks to requirements in No Child Left Behind, that's easier to do than ever before.

Let's say, for instance, that you want to know how well white students perform at these various schools.[5] Table 2 shows how this looks for the five schools near us.

Four of the five schools boast passing rates for white students that are sky-high. (Cresthaven doesn't have enough white students to be included in this measure.) That's a promising indicator. But it's also a bit misleading, because Maryland's tests, like those of most states, are easy. More than 90 percent of white students statewide pass the reading and math tests, so these schools are better than average, but not necessarily by much.

Let's dig one layer deeper. Under the No Child Left Behind Act, states have to publish test score results at three different levels: basic (below passing, but on the way there), proficient (or passing), and advanced. In a state like Maryland, where it's quite easy to score proficient, a more telling indicator is to find out how many white or middle-class students performed at the advanced level. So now let's see how our five schools look in table 3:

The plot thickens. Suddenly Woodlin doesn't look so impressive, and Piney Branch really stands out. Its average test scores might not be so great, but its white students are knocking it out of the park. Sligo Creek and Pine Crest are not far behind.

Still, I couldn't help but wonder: How do white kids in the wealthier side of the school district perform? If 100 percent of *their* white students are scoring at the advanced level, I might want to pick up and move. Remember Wood Acres Elementary from the introduction? The school in progressive, affluent Bethesda that is 84 percent white and serves a minuscule proportion of poor students? Let's see how it looks:

Table 4. Wood Acres Elementary, by White Advanced Rate

School	White Students at Advanced in Reading	White Students at Advanced in Math	GreatSchools Rating	Percent Low-Income	Percent White
Wood Acres Elementary	62%	60%	9	<1%	84%

Source: GreatSchools.org.

Ha! Is that the best you've got?

■ ■ ■

I've learned enough to convince me that these five schools are all worth considering (and that passing rates on state tests are terribly misleading). Still, I'm curious about what I'm seeing in the data. Why does Piney Branch seem to be doing so well? What about Sligo Creek and Pine Crest?

The success of Piney Branch, a school that serves third through fifth graders, might be explained in large part because its feeder school (serving Kindergarten through second grade) has a gifted and talented magnet program that attracts high-scoring out-of-boundary students.

And what about Sligo Creek and Pine Crest? Both host magnet programs that are attracting academically talented youngsters from elsewhere in the county: at Sligo Creek, a French immersion program, and at Pine Crest, an extremely competitive program for "highly gifted" children. Consider this: Only 23 percent of white Pine Crest third graders score at the advanced level in reading, while 76 percent of fourth graders and 95 percent of fifth graders do. Why the discrepancy? It's quite simple: The highly gifted program doesn't start until fourth grade.

All of this should give you one big overriding message: More than anything, test scores reflect the student demographics of a school.[6] But that doesn't mean they are immutable. A truly great school takes the pupils and families it serves and brings out the best in them. And the only way to know if a school is great by this definition is to go and check it out.

Visiting a School

The minute I walked into Piney Branch Elementary School, our local school for third through fifth grades, it failed the gut test. The hulking, 1970s-era brick building looked more like a prison than a joyful place of learning. There was nothing warm about its cinder block foyer; I've been in caves that had more light. And then there was the noise: screams and shrieks that you could imagine emanating from a Justin Bieber concert, or maybe a cockfight.

I walked into the main office, where a no-nonsense receptionist told me to take a seat. I asked her about the noise. "Is that gym class?"

"That's lunch," she said with a shrug.

After lunch, the pandemonium spilled into the hallway, as students were marshaled back to class. (In fairness, it was Halloween, and the kids were looking forward to afternoon parades and parties.) Three boisterous boys tumbled into the office, each telling the receptionist his version of the story of a fistfight that had just ensued. Within seconds they were whisked into a counselor's quarters; it was pretty clear to me that this wasn't their first visit.

Then a woman came into the office to make an announcement over the intercom. "Any children who need to borrow a Halloween costume may now come to the main office." That's a nice gesture, I thought—for a high-poverty school.

That's when it hit me: This didn't feel like a middle-class school with a few poor kids. It felt like an inner-city school that happened to be located in a middle-class community

■ ■ ■

Bertram "Mr. G." Generlette has the friendly, laid-back manner of his native Antigua. Now in his seventh year as the principal of Piney Branch, he's no stranger to Takoma Park. He attended college less than a mile from the school, at Washington Adventist University, a local Seventh-Day Adventist school founded to train missionaries, and did his student teaching at Piney Branch too. But he spent the intervening decades "up-county," first in Rockville, Maryland, as a math teacher, and then in the school district's central office.

By all accounts, he's happy to be back at Piney Branch, and has taken firm control of the school in a way that belies his relaxed style. Over 80 percent of the teachers are new since his arrival, and all of them "have bought into the vision of valuing diversity, using it as an advantage," he told me. Four of the school's nineteen classroom teachers are black (as is Mr. G), three are Hispanic, and one is Asian. He admitted that these numbers don't reflect the school's student population—65 percent of the students are black or Hispanic, including immigrants from Ethiopia, Eritrea, El Salvador, and Puerto Rico—but they are a lot better than they used to be.

As we sat down in his office, I cut right to the chase. I'm writing a book about diverse schools, I told him, but I'm also a parent, and I'm wondering if I'd be making a mistake to send my son to a school like Piney Branch. Is it going to slow him down if his classmates are several years behind or still learning the language?

It was obvious that Mr. G had heard these questions before, particularly from white folks like me. "Parents come in, yes," he told me. "They are new to the neighborhood. Or their child is in Kindergarten, or they are moving from private school. After a few minutes, you get the idea." However, he said with a sly grin, "They very rarely ask the question directly."

But he wasn't afraid to answer me directly. "We are committed to diversity," he started. "It's a lens through which we see everything. We look at test scores. How are students overall? And how are different groups doing? It's easy to see. Our white students are performing high. What can we do to keep pushing that performance up? For African American and Hispanic students, what can we do to make gains?"

And on that front, he's been quite successful. Since his arrival, the percentage of African American fifth graders passing the state reading test is way up, from 55 percent to 86 percent. For Hispanic children, it's up from 46 percent to 90 percent. Sure, it's possible that the test got easier, or the school learned how to game it, but still, these are huge improvements.

And white students' performance jumped too. Before Mr. G arrived, 33 percent of white fifth graders reached the advanced level on the state math test; in 2011, twice that number did. At Piney Branch, it appears that a rising tide is lifting all boats.

What's his secret? Was he eliminating class time for subjects not tested under No Child Left Behind, as some other local schools have done? "Not at Piney Branch," he insisted. "We still have a full science and social studies block." Was he grouping students homogeneously, so all the high-achieving kids learned together, and the slower kids got extra help? (The research we explored in Chapter Two showed mixed classrooms to be harmful to the most gifted kids.)

"There's no such thing as a homogenous group," Mr. G shot back. "One kid is a homogeneous group. As soon as you bring another student in, you have differences. The question is: How do you capitalize on the differences?"

Well, that sounds okay in theory. But come on, Mr. G, how are you going make sure *my* kid doesn't get slowed down?

"My job as a principal is to let my parents know that your child will get the services they need," he answered patiently. "We are going to make sure that every child is getting pushed to a maximum level. That's my commitment. My job is to make sure your child is achieving to the fullest extent."

And that's when I was introduced to the incredibly nuanced and elaborate efforts that Piney Branch makes to differentiate instruction, challenge every child, and avoid any appearance of segregated classrooms. First, every homeroom has a mixed group of students—the kids are assigned to make sure that every class represents the diversity of the school in terms of achievement level, race, class, and so forth. Then, during the ninety-minute reading block, students spend much of their time in small groups appropriate to their reading levels. This is nothing new; kids have been divided into "redbird" and "bluebird" reading groups for ages. However, in the new lingo of differentiated instruction, the staff works hard to make sure these groups are "fluid"—a child in a slower reading group can get bumped up to a faster one once he or she makes progress. This ensures students are taught at their level, but also that groups don't break down entirely by race and class.

For math, on the other hand, students are split up into homogeneous classrooms. Mr. G says that because of the way math is taught—with each new skill often building off an understanding of the last—it's hard to teach kids of wildly different performance levels at the same time. All the advanced math kids in a grade are in one classroom, the middle students in another, and the struggling kids in a third. This means shuffling students between rooms, which can be quite time-consuming for elementary school kids. And yes, it also means that most of the white students are together in the top class (though not all of the school's high achievers are white). But it allows the highest-performing kids to sprint ahead; one of the school's third-grade math classes, for example, is tackling the district's fifth-grade math curriculum.

The rest of the time—when kids are learning science or social studies or taking "specials" like art and music—they are back in their heterogeneous classrooms. Even then, however, teachers work to differentiate instruction, which often means separating the kids back into groups again, and offering more challenging, extended assignments to the higher-achieving students.

It sounds like some sort of elaborately choreographed dance to me, but it appears to succeed on several counts. All kids spend most of the day getting challenged at their own levels—and no one ever sits in a classroom that's entirely segregated by race or class.

The test scores indicate that the strategy is working, but that doesn't mean all parents have been thrilled. Three years ago, Mr. G told me, a group of parents pushed to get the school to move to homogeneous classrooms for reading, as well as math. "Parents felt that the only way to get kids to read at a high level was to have other kids around them who read at a high level," he explained. (That didn't sound so unreasonable to me.) "We had a lot of meetings. The staff overwhelmingly supported the diverse approach, the heterogeneous approach. That was good for me as an administrator, because the staff was behind me. If the parents wanted that kind of philosophy, they would go to another school. There are lots of schools where they could do that."

I tracked down one of the critical parents, Susan Katz Miller. Miller personifies much of what makes Takoma Park great: She's smart, she's an activist, and she's committed to helping make the city a welcoming community for families of all incomes and backgrounds. A neighbor of mine called her "a force of nature." A former *Newsweek* reporter and now a columnist for the

Takoma Voice, she spent three years as PTA president at Piney Branch and is an enthusiastic booster of the school and its diversity. "My kids have both benefited enormously from being in a Piney Branch social milieu," she told me.

But the reading decision still sticks in her craw. "Why is it okay," she asked, "to have homogeneous grouping in math and not have it in reading? The answer you get is: 'Well, we can't do both, they would be switching classes all the time, it would be like middle school, and they won't be able to handle it.'" But in her view, "It's a huge disservice to the kids who are ready for rigor in the humanities and are not math kids. It's bizarre. We've said we're going to accommodate kids in math but not in reading. It's completely insane, as far as I'm concerned."

Miller lost that battle, but Mr. G and his teachers didn't ignore the parents' concerns, either. The district was rolling out reading programs suitable for advanced students, and Mr. G made sure his teachers were trained in them, so that the students in the top reading groups would be challenged with difficult material. He tried hard to live up to his promise to push all students as far as they could go, and the teachers loved the new programs.

Mr. G and Piney Branch also faced some healthy competition. Montgomery County offers seven centers for the highly gifted—magnet schools for super-smart fourth and fifth graders, located in elementary buildings throughout the district. As I mentioned, Pine Crest, just a few miles away from Piney Branch, hosts one such center, and an increasing number of Piney Branch third graders were testing into it for fourth and fifth grades.

In 2009, twenty-five Piney Branch kids, most of them white or Asian, were accepted—more than from any other elementary school in the district. If they all took up the offer and left, Mr. G said, "That's a teacher walking out of my building." (Roughly one teacher is assigned for every twenty-five students.)

So in 2009–10, in cooperation with the district and at the urging of the parents, Piney Branch launched a pilot program to bring the highly gifted centers' curriculum into its classrooms. This wasn't easy; there really wasn't a curriculum, per se, at the centers. Teachers had the freedom to teach what they wanted. So the district helped the teachers put down on paper everything they were doing in the classroom.

Mr. G made sure that two of his teachers, one in fourth grade and one in fifth, were trained on the highly gifted approaches, and those teachers subsequently formed groups of advanced students in their classroom. In those classrooms, there are twelve or so highly gifted students, and another twelve or so students closer to grade level. While they are taught together some of the day, they are frequently broken into small groups, so the highly gifted kids can learn together at an accelerated pace.

Pulling this off takes an energetic and gifted educator. Fourth-grade teacher Folakemi Mosadomi—who has the highly gifted group in her classroom—appears to fit the bill perfectly. Now in her seventh year of teaching, all of them at Piney Branch, Ms. M, as she is called, acknowledged that differentiating instruction in this way requires "extensive planning and training," not to mention creativity and strong organization. But even that's not always enough.

In the first year of the pilot, she had four different reading groups in one classroom, from kids still learning English to the highly gifted students. "I went from sounding out the 'A' sound with one group to talking to another group about how the Exxon Valdez oil spill was like the Battle of Normandy." That range was simply too much for one teacher to handle—remember Caroline Hoxby's research that the variance in student skills in one classroom shouldn't be too great?—so the next year Ms. M had just two groups: the highly gifted students, and the next level down. "Now it's easier to do more with both groups of students together," she told me.

And the strategy seems to be working in one important way: The year after that switch was made, about half of the highly gifted children chose to stay at Piney Branch.

But Do the Kids Hang Out Together?

I was convinced that Piney Branch is making heroic efforts to challenge all of its students while maintaining and honoring its diversity. That addresses at least three-quarters of my concerns. But the other quarter is cultural: What does the school *feel* like? Do children of different races play together at recess?

Do their parents work together? Does the school's diversity extend beyond its classrooms? Are there racial or class tensions?

Mr. G admitted that the school faces challenges on this front. He notices some self-segregation on the playground, for instance, as when the African American kids are step-dancing and white students feel excluded. Ms. M sees the other side of the same problem: many of the highly gifted white students sitting together and reading.

Getting parents to socialize across racial and class lines isn't easy, either. The leadership of the school's PTA is predominantly white, though it includes a few African Americans. Mr. G is working hard to make all families feel welcome and empowered, though. For instance, he invited Impact Silver Spring, a local grassroots organization, to hold training sessions at the school to teach families how to be more involved in their kids' education, and to develop a cohort of minority parents that feels comfortable attending school functions together.

To see for myself what the interactions were like, I showed up at a PTA meeting. It was an incredibly informative experience; I would strongly recommend doing the same for any school you are considering for your child. The meeting was relatively well attended, with about three dozen parents filling the school's cafeteria. As Mr. G indicated, most of the parents where white, though perhaps a half-dozen were people of color.

The next day I spoke with Adrienne Tilton, the co-president of the PTA. A friendly mother of four, with sandy brown hair pulled back in a ponytail, she admitted that the PTA is not as diverse as the school. "I don't know why that is, necessarily," she said. As she thought about it, she acknowledged, "When you're recruiting people or talking people up, you're talking to people you know and see every day." Those tend to be people of the same socioeconomic status. She also relayed some conversations she'd had with Latino parents; in their home countries they simply dropped off their kids at school and picked them up. To do more would be to show disrespect to the professional educators.

I asked Tilton how the diversity is working out for the school's students. She was strongly supportive of the mixed classrooms. "Do you really want your kid to go to a school where the kids who live in apartment buildings are all in this classroom? The kids who have houses all go to this classroom? And we never see or talk to each other?" An elegant way of putting it, I thought. But do the kids hang out together after school?

Tilton said her son has made diverse friends at Piney Branch, and she's glad for that. Those friendships only go so far, though. "We don't really see them on the weekends or play much after school," she said. "The kids he plays with are the kids he went to preschool with."

Ask the Tough Questions

Now you see how one school handles issues related to diversity. More importantly, you should have a feel for the kinds of questions you might ask as you check out a school. Granted, I was fortunate to have my writer's hat on as I did so, which gave me permission to have conversations with the principal, teachers, and others that might be more awkward for a typical parent. But if you want to find out whether a diverse school is right for you and your child, you need to be willing to ask many of these same questions, too.

Probably the most important thing to learn is whether the principal is a strong leader and open to tackling these vexing issues of race and class head-on. After all, it takes an extraordinary person to bring together students, teachers, and parents of diverse cultures and backgrounds and make the mix work effectively. It especially requires a ton of outreach and communication on the leader's part. Is the principal up to this task? Does he or she even see it as part of the job? If not, that's a big red flag. And if you are treated like a pushy parent for just trying to find out, go somewhere else, fast.

Second, you want to understand the school's instructional strategies, particularly when it comes to serving kids who are achieving at vastly different levels. How does it group students, and how are students selected for those groups? Do the groups change much over time? If the school uses mixed grouping, how does it challenge all of its students, especially the highest-achieving ones? Likewise, what is it doing to boost the performance of its struggling students? If the school says it differentiates instruction, what evidence is there that this is for real, and that teachers are up to the challenge? Ask to see the different kinds of assignments that teachers give to kids at different levels. If the school can't provide such examples, that's another red flag. At the middle and high school levels, does the school offer honors tracks or Advanced Placement courses?

Third, you want to learn how integrated the school truly is. Is there a lot of self-segregation at recess and lunch? Are people of color represented at PTA meetings? Are parents chatting with moms and dads of different races? What schoolwide events are hosted to make people feel included? Is there an International Night? School fairs?

Finally, trust your gut. But also be willing to admit that your gut can sometimes be wrong.

Expanding Your Options: Magnet and Charter Schools

As I alluded to earlier, parents in most big cities can choose schools outside of their own neighborhoods. Let me offer a few words on the most common of these public schools of choice, magnets and charters.

Magnet schools, first conceived in the desegregation era of the 1970s, are designed to attract white and/or affluent parents to schools in tough parts of town, through specialized programs like Montessori, language immersion, or math and science. Many magnets also use selective admissions processes, accepting students on the basis of their test scores or other indicators, such as their artistic talents. In lots of big cities, magnets are the only schools with any real racial or socioeconomic diversity.

Still, magnet schools aren't perfect solutions to the Diverse Schools Dilemma. As Boston University political scientist Christine Rossell has explained, the most common magnet programs are schools within schools.[7] Pine Crest Elementary's highly gifted program is a good example. The school's "regular" student population is almost entirely Latino and low-income, but its magnet program is overwhelmingly white, Asian, and affluent. The school looks integrated on paper, but in reality there are two separate schools operating under one roof—and neither one has a very diverse mix of students.

Such stories are not unusual. Another school in my area, Eastern Middle, also has a regular student body that is overwhelmingly poor and Hispanic. But its acclaimed humanities and communications program—which students around Montgomery County compete to get into—is overwhelmingly white (and female). That wouldn't be so bad if the school worked to create opportunities whereby students from different backgrounds might mix and get to know one another. But such opportunities are few and far between.

"I don't think I've ever seen that kind of a gulf between two groups within the same school," said Nick Nathanson, a Takoma Park parent whose daughter attended the humanities magnet. "It isn't a hostility or warfare or conflict. It's just that the two groups by and large go about their very different business entirely separately. There just doesn't seem to be any mixing at all in classes, in the cafeteria, or outside of school between the magnet kids and the neighborhood kids."

A better model—and one that is generally more popular with parents—is the "whole school" magnet, in which all of the students travel to the school and participate in the same instructional program. But these are exceedingly rare, because, as Rossell explains, "creating them requires that an entire school be emptied out and children assigned elsewhere or a new school be built."[8]

Enter charter schools. Charter schools are public schools of choice that operate independently from school districts and are generally outside the bounds of restrictive teacher-union contracts. Like magnet schools, most adopt special themes or philosophies that draw niche groups of students and teachers alike. But unlike magnets, most charters are started from scratch, with new staff and students. Furthermore, they aren't allowed to have entrance requirements. There are virtually no charter schools that students must test into; instead, popular ones hold a lottery for admission.

For better or worse, most charter schools serve a high-poverty, high-minority population. (In many states charters are allowed to operate only in "failing" urban districts.) But some charter schools are pursuing integration with success. They have certain advantages: As start-up schools, they can be strategic about their locations, and pick spots that are well positioned to draw students from different racial and socioeconomic groups. They can also design academic programs that take diversity as a given and make the most of it. And they can be thoughtful about putting elements in place that will appeal to whites and blacks, Asians and Hispanics, rich and poor alike.

Capital City Public Charter School, located on the boundary between the rapidly gentrifying Adams Morgan, Mount Pleasant, and Columbia Heights neighborhoods in Washington, D.C., is one such school. It serves pre-Kindergarten through seventh-grade students from almost every zip code in the city, which helps it achieve a nearly even racial and socioeconomic balance. One-third of its pupils are white, another third black, and most of the rest Hispanic; nearly half of its students qualify for a free or reduced-price lunch. The school occupies a renovated church building with bright walls and a warm, welcoming feel. Perhaps these visuals help to explain why Cap City was the very first school that Barack and Michelle Obama visited as president and first lady. (Its proximity to the White House probably didn't hurt, either.)

Capital City, founded in 2000, is a proudly progressive school; it uses an Outward Bound expeditionary learning approach that takes students into the community. This is a big attraction for many parents, especially the more affluent ones. But there's a historical reason, too, that the school has been able to attract affluent white families and maintain such strong racial balance: It was founded by white parents. At the time, their children attended Hearst Elementary, a public school in a ritzy Northwest D.C. neighborhood. The parents became upset when a new superintendent imposed an unfriendly principal on their school and transferred some of their best teachers elsewhere. Those parents recruited one of the teachers, Karen Dresden, to run the charter school; she's still running it today, and credits the parents for having the vision to create a diverse school. "What I was really impressed with was they were committed from the very beginning to creating a school not just for their own kids to attend, but for all children," Dresden said.

The school's location was critically important, too. Like many charters, Cap City had to scramble to find available space; it settled on a commercial facility a few blocks from its current location. Ten years ago, Dresden said, "This was really a rocky area. It was all vacant lots; it wasn't developed like it is now. When we decided to locate the school here there were a couple members of the founding group who decided for various reasons that they did not want their kid to come here. I think they were feeling a little too unsafe. But that was actually a really good thing. The people who were really committed to it said, 'This is where we're going to have the most diversity.'"

The first year, the school's population was about 50 percent black, 25 percent Hispanic, and 25 percent white. Until then, virtually all D.C. charters had been 100 percent minority.

Now Cap City has such a strong reputation that it doesn't have to worry about recruiting enough white and middle-class students. There is a mile-long waiting list of children from nearby Adams Morgan and from farther-away neighborhoods like Capitol Hill and Chevy Chase. "There are families choosing Capital City today that would have never chosen it when we started," Dresden told me. The school's bigger problem is making sure that enough low-income and minority students enter its lottery. To that end, the school does an enormous amount of outreach in Latino and African American communities.

At the other end of the educational spectrum from Cap City is the Denver School of Science and Technology. The original DSST is a middle and high school located in the trendy, mixed-income Stapleton neighborhood, where the old Denver airport used to be. Almost 70 percent of its students are African American or Hispanic, and 40 percent of its 2009 graduating class was first-generation college-bound. Yet it's the highest-performing school in Denver, hands down. Its students, many of whom enter the school at least a grade level behind, are making huge gains on standardized tests. Perhaps most impressively, 100 percent of the school's first senior class was accepted into four-year colleges, including Stanford, MIT, Caltech, and Wesleyan.

Those impressive results mean that DSST is now luring affluent families away from Denver's most selective private schools. "We've made a whole group of upper-middle-class parents in town reconsider public education," Bill Kurtz, the school's founder, told me. But that doesn't mean DSST is for everyone. Some white parents, he said, take a look at the school's daily assembly, gulp, and say that they didn't know that most students were minorities. Furthermore, Kurtz said, "There's a segment of the population who would want progressive, project-based learning who would not come here."

That type of parent might be taken aback by the fact that the kids wear uniforms, and walk silently in the hallways. There's a lot of structure and discipline at DSST. But it's a science and technology school, so it doesn't really have to appeal to fuzzy-headed humanities types like me. Those who buy into rigorous standards and a college-prep curriculum, whatever their race or economic class, will be thrilled. Because of DSST's success, Kurtz said, "People want their kids in a great public school. They are willing to sacrifice touchy-feely stuff."

So what's the downside of high-quality charter schools? They must admit students by lottery, which means that there's no guarantee that you'll get into your school of choice. Talk about an anxiety-producing situation! Many D.C. parents I know decided to enter a charter school lottery, and when their kids didn't get selected, they started looking for a home in the suburbs the next day.

But there's another approach besides packing your bags: Stick around, and try to improve the school you've been dealt.

Endnotes

1   The Coleman Report found the tipping point to be 40 percent poor. That's the guideline used by some school districts when they seek to keep their schools economically balanced. Clearly, this is not an exact science.

2   Judith Anderson, Debra Hollinger, and Joseph Conaty, *Poverty and Achievement: Re-examining the Relationship between School Poverty and Student Achievement: An Examination of Eighth Grade Student Achievement Using the National Education Longitudinal Study of 1988* (Washington, D.C.: U.S. Department of Education, 1992), 2–5; David Rusk, "To Improve Public Education, Stop Moving Money," *Abell Report* 11, no. 2 (1998): 6–7. Both cited in Kahlenberg, *All Together Now*, 40.

3   This figure is based on the author's own calculations using the federal Common Core of Data, National Center for Education Statistics, http://nces.ed.gov/ccd/index.asp.

4   Charles T. Clotfelter, *After Brown: The Rise and Retreat of School Desegregation* (Princeton, NJ: Princeton University Press, 2004), 110–14.

5   It's actually hard to find data in some states for the performance of "non-poor" students. So you might have to settle for "white" as the closest proxy. One hopes that this exercise will get easier in the future, as states improve their data systems.

6   Most states are moving to a "growth" model, which examines the progress a school's students each make over the course of the year. This is a much better indicator of the

impact of the school than the metrics that have been used till now, which essentially just measure whether or not students pass the test. However, from a parent's perspective, you still want to know how high- (or low-) performing your child's potential peers are going to be. So ideally you'd look at both static test scores and "growth" indicators. That should be easier to do in the years ahead.

7   Christine H. Rossell, "Magnet Schools: No Longer Famous but Still Intact," *Education Next* 5, no. 2 (2005): 44–49.

8   Ibid., 46.

5

How to Gentrify a High-Poverty Public School

The demographics of many of America's urban centers are changing rapidly. Whereas the cities of the mid-1950s were marked by extreme segregation, today's are more integrated than at any time since 1910. One recent analysis reports that only one in five African Americans currently lives in a neighborhood that is at least 80 percent black, compared to nearly one in two fifty years ago.[1]

While gentrification doesn't entirely explain the trend—the outmigration of African American families to the suburbs and to warmer climes is a more significant factor—several of our great cities are seeing a historic number of white and/or affluent families returning, and staying.

As discussed in the introduction, what's most notable about the last half decade is that more of these families are choosing to send their children to the public schools—turning some of those schools from all black to "mocha," as one commentator put it.[2] This development holds great promise in terms of integrating our schools. But as with so many issues related to race and class, it also has the potential to become a tinderbox. Let's take a closer look, particularly for middle-class parents who might participate in the gentrification of a high-poverty public school.

"Tipping In"

As a doctoral candidate at Columbia University's Teachers College, Jennifer Burns Stillman wrote a dissertation weaving together three of her interests: parenting (she's the mother of two small children), gentrification (she's lived in three rapidly changing neighborhoods in New York City), and education (she's a former high school social studies teacher).

Her dissertation was recently published as a book, *Gentrification and Schools: The Process of Integration When Whites Reverse Flight.* In it, she offers a scholarly look at the changes underway at a handful of New York City elementary schools, and an in-depth look at the white, middle-class parents at the center of the story.[3]

As a white, middle-class mother herself, she's sympathetic to the "gentry parents," as she calls them, who "tip in" to high-poverty schools. (She contrasts this with what economist Thomas Schelling called the "tipping out" of white families in the 1960s and '70s.) But she's not blind to the wrenching, disruptive nature of the changes rocking these neighborhoods, and what it means for longtime residents. Nonetheless, she's hopeful that the process of white flight in reverse might lead to diverse public schools, benefitting students of all classes and races.

What Stillman chronicles is a process of school gentrification with several distinct phases. First, a handful of white, middle-class parents—often foreigners—send their children to what was previously a high-poverty, all-minority school. These "innovators," as Stillman labels them, break the color barrier. A few more "early adopter" parents join them, and together they recruit an "early majority" of middle-class peers (often through organized efforts over a community listserve). Many of these parents eventually wash out of the school, scared off by the challenges associated with gentrification. But if enough can be encouraged to stay—and if more middle-class parents are recruited to replace the ones who left—then the school can be integrated. Voila!

Of course, it's not that simple. All diverse schools must manage the kind of cultural conflicts we discussed in Chapter Three, but these conflicts are all the more charged—racially, socioeconomically—when the school is going through a demographic shift.

For example, Stillman told the story of one group of affluent New York City parents who turned their dinner-party angst over whether to send their kids to the neighborhood public school into an organized effort to gentrify it. They created an organization to raise money for the school and to encourage local parents to consider sending their children there.

Granted, these parents weren't a part of the school community yet; their children were still toddlers and preschoolers. And they recognized that a group of affluent, mostly white parents raising money and pushing for changes at the school might set off all kinds of alarm bells among the minority community and school leadership. As one dad explained to Stillman, the group tried to be mindful of the community and avoid coded language. Above all, they didn't want to be perceived as racist.

But their plan didn't work, especially when it came to the school's black principal. According to Stillman,

> Dr. Caraway, described by many as "paranoid," unleashed a fury. None of the [gentry parents] that I spoke to could pinpoint exactly what her grievances were with the group—race? class? attitudes? tactics?—they just perceived that she was not open to a new demographic shaking things up in her school.[4]

Stillman later wrote, "Dr. Caraway was 'ousted' or 'retired,' depending on who is telling the story."

Was Caraway right to be paranoid? Stillman described several schools where the new parents started pushing for progressive pedagogical approaches that, as we learned in Chapter Three, might have been good for their kids, but not for many of the poor children there already. She quoted many white, middle-class parents expressing concerns that their neighborhood school was "too traditional" or did "too much test prep." "I just want something more interesting for my child," one mother, a poet, explained.[5]

Caraway was also worried about losing Title I money—federal funds that flow to schools with high proportions of poor children. Indeed, some of the schools in Stillman's study did lose their Title I grants, whose funds had been used to support smaller class sizes. The newly arrived parents could offset some of the losses with fundraising, but it was hard to make up for them entirely.

The toughest issues came down to different approaches to childrearing, as the sociologist Annette Lareau might have predicted. A notable flash point was "the unbearable norm of 'yelling' adults," Stillman wrote. The parents she interviewed said that everywhere they looked, they saw teachers, administrators, aides, and parents yelling at young children. One parent who had left a gentrifying school explained her decision to Stillman: "I do think it is a little strange when you're walking down the halls of the school and you hear teachers shouting and screaming 'Shut up!' at the kids."[6]

Yet for all of these challenges, the social mixing that integrated schools afford was powerful, for both parents and children. One middle-class parent told Stillman about how collaborating on fundraisers with less affluent but no less dedicated moms changed her own perceptions. "It really has sort of become a much less divided kind of world for me, which has been very nice," she told Stillman. As for the children, Stillman wrote, they "didn't seem to have a problem; mixing came easy."[7]

Gentrifying Schools in Washington, D.C.

The demographic transitions Stillman detailed in New York City can also be spotted four hours south, in Washington.

Consider the saga at Ludlow-Taylor, an elementary school near Capitol Hill's H Street corridor that was following in the footsteps of Maury, the school profiled in the introduction. In 2008, a group of middle-class preschool parents in the school's catchment zone organized a meeting with then–schools chancellor Michelle Rhee, who was the first non-black head of D.C. schools in decades. Flyers were posted announcing a meeting to discuss making Ludlow-Taylor a "community-based school" again. Those signs were read by many black families as white code for "let's take over this school."

The meeting was extraordinarily contentious, with hostility between the mostly white "Friends of Ludlow-Taylor" group and the all-black group of current Ludlow-Taylor parents on full display. One local parent posted this on his blog:

> I'm freaked out, I don't know that I've ever been a part of a large-scale meeting or conversation that so accurately reflected our current national debate on race, class, education, and gentrification. All the usual suspects were there: well meaning White liberals who "just want to help," outraged parents of current students (current stats show that NO children classified as "White" attend LT, take that for what it's worth), and teachers & administrators caught between the two groups.

After providing a play-by-play of the forum, he went on to write:

> Let's be serious shall we? It's obvious that the members of [Friends of Ludlow-Taylor] are working off the standard model of participation (The Peace Corps, Teach for America, VISTA, etc.) for White people who "want to make a difference." Swoop in with the ink just barely dry on their diplomas, do some stuff that doesn't affect the structural/institutional forces that created the conditions they're trying to correct, and then leave feeling good about themselves. All the while completely ignoring the input and experiences of the people they're allegedly there to "help."[8]

Rhee soon assigned a new principal to the school and the gentrification process went forward; white students are now 10 percent of the school's total enrollment.

Tensions flared again in 2009 in another part of the city regarding Hardy Middle School, which, though located in affluent, white Georgetown, served a predominantly African American population from elsewhere in the city. Rhee, who wanted to draw more neighborhood families to the school, told a gathering of mostly white parents that Hardy was going to become a more attractive option for them, but it wasn't going to "turn" overnight. "If you're a civil rights lawyer and you read that, you're asking, 'Turn from what to what? Turn from who to who?'" Keenan Keller, whose daughter attended Hardy, told the *Washington Post*.[9]

At Maury, Heather Schoell said, everyone has focused on keeping these kinds of polarized dynamics from playing out. "We have worked really hard to go slowly, take small steps, so that our school can grow and thrive without leaving anyone out or making people feel like they can't go there anymore. That has been something that we've been very conscious of and very careful about. While we want to grow and we want to thrive, it's almost not as important as keeping that family and neighborhood feel to the school."

So, for example, the PTA hosts an annual talent show and silent auction fundraiser—but sets the admissions price at five dollars so everyone can attend. And parents who can't afford even that much are discreetly comped. (Fundraisers are certainly a sensitive area. According to a March 2012 *New York Times* article, expensive fundraising events and even bake-sale price increases can alienate poorer families.[10])

Another Capitol Hill school, Brent Elementary, has also been managing its change process carefully, working to ensure that nobody feels threatened. So many of its parents were outraged in 2011 when a *Washington Examiner* columnist printed an essay arguing that black families were being "pushed out."

> Some black parents are not pleased about the white influx. An unintended consequence of schools improving and drawing white students is that blacks are forced out in some cases. Take Brent Elementary on Capitol Hill. Black families drove their children across the river from Anacostia for a better education. They were out of boundary. Now white families near Brent are filling the classrooms. There's no room for the Anacostia kids, who have essentially been pushed out—after investing in the school.[11]

As the white parents pointed out, all students at Brent have a right to stay there until they graduate. Nobody is literally "pushed out." Still, with a mostly black fifth-grade class, and mostly white preschoolers, there's little doubt that Brent is changing, and fast. Within a few years, it won't be serving any Anacostia youngsters.

From "Tipping In" to Tipping Over

The Brent experience raises a vexing issue: What happens when a school integrates but then keeps on changing? What if the school fully flips, from all black to all white or mostly poor to mostly affluent?

Ross Elementary is a case in point. An intimate little school in Washington's Dupont Circle neighborhood, for years it served a predominantly African American and Hispanic population of out-of-boundary students. Its local community—a mix of affluent gays, young urban professionals, and diplomats—didn't have many children, and those who did generally sent them to private schools. Nor did the school seem all that interested in attracting neighborhood students anyway. "The word we got from the principal," said Eric Akridge, a local stay-at-home-dad, "was, 'I'm not really interested in parent involvement.' What she was really saying to members of the in-boundary community was, 'I'm really not interested in your kid.'"

That all changed in the course of a few years. The longtime principal retired and was replaced by a new leader who reached out to the community. (Remember what I said about the importance of the school principal?) Then, in 2007, Michelle Rhee stormed into town as Washington's chancellor of schools. At last, Akridge told me, "We got some fresh, non-apathetic blood into the leadership of the school."

In the fall of 2007, Akridge and his partner put their son in Ross's pre-Kindergarten program and were thrilled with its diversity. Split evenly among whites, blacks, Asians, and Hispanics, "it was about as perfect as we could have imagined." This was hugely important to them. "A key cornerstone of our decision to stay in the city was that we didn't want our kid growing up thinking that all kids had the same things that he had," he said. "That's not reflective of our world."

So far, so good. Akridge's son, now in third grade, is thriving at the school, and enjoys his classmates, who haven't changed much since his pre-K years. But Akridge sees trouble on the horizon: The preschool and Kindergarten classes are almost entirely white. He is not the only one bothered by that; this has become a big topic of discussion at the school's PTA meetings, where the consensus is that parents want to maintain the school's diversity. Akridge also senses that black families feel they are being pushed out.

In Ross's case, it's not that white neighborhood parents have finally decided to send their children to the school. The neighborhood is still largely short on kids; the new white families are mostly from out-of-boundary communities, just like the black and Latino families they replaced. But out-of-boundary placements are decided in D.C. by a blind lottery. If mostly white families enter the lottery for Ross, then mostly white families win the lottery, and the school's demographics keep changing.

The school's African American principal has been brainstorming with parents about ways to reach out to black and Latino families to encourage more of them to apply. They have targeted listserves of minority parents and plan to hold outreach meetings. But it's far from clear that any of these efforts will work; without being able to give preference to certain students in the lottery in order to maintain the school's diversity, there's a good chance that Ross will soon be as white as many of its counterparts in the suburbs.

"We like the diversity and we embrace it and we want it to continue," said Akridge. "That's why we're there." Yet that diversity is slipping away.

Solving the Collective Action Problem

Jennifer Burns Stillman writes about the collective action problem of getting enough innovators and early adopters to send their kids to a high-poverty school in order to build and sustain an early majority. But there's another collective action problem: Once changes at a school are underway, how can they be stopped from turning the building into an affluent, white enclave—especially if the surrounding neighborhood is mostly affluent and white? I can't imagine a group of white parents getting together on a listserve to volunteer *not* to send their kids to the newly gentrified school down the street.

In this case, the only viable solutions will come from public policy. One possibility is to move to some version of "controlled choice," whereby public officials work to manage enrollment at local schools in order to create more socioeconomic balance. (A Supreme Court decision a few years ago made overt management by race unallowable, but districts can still manipulate enrollment based on income.) This sort of effort comes in several flavors. Here are the major options:

1. **Eliminate the boundary system entirely.** Nobody would have a claim to a particular school, even the one down the block. (This is how it used to work in San Francisco, much to the consternation of many middle-class parents.) Everyone would apply to several schools, and a computer would determine enrollments, based on a mix of a lottery, geographic proximity, and the goal of socioeconomic balance.

2. **Redraw boundaries to engineer more schools with socioeconomic balance.** This could take a couple of different forms. If a school is near a border that separates an affluent neighborhood and a poor one, its boundaries could be drawn to ensure enrollment from both communities. Another option is to ensure that all schools have a large number of out-of-boundary slots reserved for poor kids.

3. **Create magnet schools in strategic locations to draw middle-class and poor students alike.** As explained in Chapter Four, this strategy has worked for a generation or longer, at least when officials come up with magnet schools that are worth attending. For instance, officials could turn an under-enrolled high-poverty school into a Montessori school or bilingual immersion program—offerings that are attractive to many middle-class parents. Charter schools could play this magnet role, too, but they would need to be able to manage their lotteries to ensure a balance of middle-class and low-income students—something discouraged by federal and (often) state policy today.

For parents, the takeaway is this: If you're courageous enough to be part of a school's gentrification process, be aware that you might end up displacing the poor children, rather than creating a nicely integrated school. Unless that's what you want, keep reading.

Endnotes

1   Edward Glaeser and Jacob Vigdor, *The End of the Segregated Century: Racial Separation in America's Neighborhoods, 1890–2010* (New York: Manhattan Institute for Policy Research, January 2012).

2   Harry Jaffe, "D.C. Schools See New Faces—Many of Them White," *Washington Examiner*, August 29, 2011.

3   Jennifer Burns Stillman, *Gentrification and Schools: The Process of Integration When Whites Reverse Flight* (New York: Palgrave Macmillan, 2012).

4   Ibid., XX.

5   Ibid., XX.

6   Ibid., XX.

7   Ibid., XX.

8   Hill Rat, "Community Meeting at Ludlow-Taylor (continued)," *Hill Rat*, March 20, 2008, http://hillratdc.blogspot.com/2008/03/community-meeting-at-ludlow-taylor_20.html.

9   Bill Turque, "D.C. School Uneasy about Rhee's Plans for It," *Washington Post*, November 13, 2009.

10   Kyle Spencer, "At the PTA, Clashes over Cupcakes and Culture," *New York Times*, March 16, 2012.

11   Jaffe, "D.C. Schools See New Faces."

6

Affluent Schools with Racial Diversity: The Rewards without the Risks?

Parents considering diverse schools want to minimize the risks for their children and maximize the benefits. This is how parents framed the issue in their interviews with Naomi Calvo, for her dissertation on Seattle's public school choice program:

> The positive side of diversity encompassed both cultural enrichment and the perceived benefits of having children learn how to deal with the "real world" that parents expect they will have to navigate as adults. At the same time, parents wanted to protect their children from bad peer influences, and they also worried that concentrations of disadvantaged, special education or [English as a Second Language] children would detract from their own child's learning experiences by taking up teacher time and resources. In other words, parents wanted their kids exposed to diversity but not contaminated by it. Since it is generally hard to find the positive forms of diversity without the negative aspects, and since even the positive forms involve sacrificing other desired elements, many parents placed diversity low on their list of priorities.[1]

Is Calvo right that it's hard to find "the positive forms of diversity without the negative aspects"? There's one obvious place to look: schools that predominantly serve affluent students but also boast some degree of racial diversity. Almost every city has these—public schools on the affluent side of town, selective-admissions magnet schools, and private schools. (Yes, private schools.)

Affluent, Racially Diverse Public Schools

There's much to like about racially diverse, affluent schools. They tend to be safe. They instill an expectation that students will go to college. They provide an opportunity for students to learn about cultures different from theirs. And because most of the school's parents fall in a similar income bracket, most are also likely to embrace similar values and child-rearing practices. (Remember Annette Lareau's study? Upper-middle-class black families parented the same as upper-middle-class white families did.) Perhaps best of all, achievement gaps between white and minority students tend to be much smaller in these schools than in ones that are made up only of rich white kids and poor minority kids.

That's not to say all group differences disappear even in schools that are uniformly affluent. The achievement gap between white and black students (on average, a four-year gap in reading levels by twelfth grade) can be partly explained by class differences: White kids are much less likely to be poor than black children are. But that doesn't totally account for the gap. Simply put, poor black students tend to perform worse than poor white students do, and affluent black kids tend to perform worse than affluent white kids do.[2] This can be a painful issue for racially diverse schools to grapple with, and can result in classrooms that are still segregated by race, as white students migrate toward the accelerated reading and math groups and advanced courses, and black and Hispanic kids trend toward the on-level and remedial tracks.

The most-studied example of this phenomenon is in Shaker Heights, Ohio, an affluent, progressive, racially integrated suburb of Cleveland. The late ethnographer John Ogbu, a native of Nigeria, spent four months living and working in Shaker Heights at the request of its black community, which sought an explanation for the academic disengagement exhibited by many of its affluent children and their subsequent low test scores and grade point averages. He identified several systemic barriers to black achievement, but his most provocative, and controversial, finding was this:

> From our observations in almost every schoolwork situation, our discussion with groups of students and school personnel, and our interviews, we can confidently say that Black students in Shaker Heights from elementary school through high school did not work as hard as they should and could to make better grades than their records show. The students themselves knew and admitted this.[3]

Ogbu, and dozens of other scholars, have hypothesized why this might be so. One explanation is that black students sense that white students and teachers think they aren't smart, or at least not "book smart," and they eventually internalize this belief. (Sociologists call this "stereotype threat.") Or that African American students—especially teenage boys—who do well in school get teased by their friends for "acting white." Or that black parents allow their kids to watch too much TV or don't make them do their homework. Or that the most prominent black role models are sports and entertainment stars whose success had nothing to do with academic achievement. (Of course, President Obama's election has put a significant dent in that excuse. And he addresses the issue virtually every time he speaks to a black audience.)

Ogbu was convinced that the "acting white" issue was a serious one, a perspective later confirmed by other scholars. Roland Fryer, an African American Harvard economist and recipient of a MacArthur "genius" grant, figured out a way to measure the popularity of high school students. He combined that measure with student outcomes and found that for white students, the higher their GPA, the more friends they had. But for black and Hispanic students, it was the opposite: High-achieving students paid a social price for doing well in school, and the lower-performing kids had the most friends. This was particularly true for adolescent boys, especially in integrated schools. (Fryer didn't see evidence of pressure against "acting white" in all-minority schools.) This finding, he wrote, "adds to the evidence of a 'Shaker Heights' syndrome, in which racially integrated settings only reinforce pressures to toe the ethnic line."[4]

So how do affluent diverse schools handle the achievement gap and "acting white" issues? Let's visit one such school that's a stone's throw from Washington, D.C.

Bethesda-Chevy Chase High School, Montgomery County, Maryland

This first thing that Bethesda-Chevy Chase principal Karen Lockard wanted me to know about her school is that it's no elite bastion of affluence. "It's very easy to look at us and look at the real estate and look at the zip codes that come here and say that we are an affluent, high-achieving school," she told me. "And we are that school." But it's more complicated than that. "We've got the ambassadors' kids, and we've got their maids' kids."

If you want to find the beau ideal of a "common school"—and judging by the frequency of TV camera crews that visit the school, the major national networks certainly do—it's hard to beat B-CC. Children of Washington's elite who live in two-million-dollar homes rub shoulders with kids who came from El Salvador just months ago and don't know how to read or write in any language. Throw in a sizable group of upper-middle-class African American and Latino children, plus a plethora of international kids (of all races) whose parents work at the World Bank, along with plenty of white middle-class kids and some poor black and Hispanic kids, and you have a pretty interesting social experiment, all housed in a handsome, newly renovated building just blocks from Bethesda's thriving downtown.

By and large, the experiment seems to be working well. The school's enrollment is way up, climbing from about 1,000 in the late 1990s to about 1,800 today. It's ranked #145 on *Newsweek*'s list of the best high schools in the country. And as Matt Gandal, an Education Department official and the president of the B-CC Foundation, told me, the school "has a reputation for honoring diversity without sacrificing quality."

In fact, the school is so hot that it is effectively luring families back from Washington's high-priced private schools, especially during the Great Recession. B-CC's freshman class in the fall of 2009 was at least one hundred students larger than the class of eighth graders who graduated from its feeder middle school the previous spring. "Now you tell me where else these kids came from, if not from private schools," Lockard said. Later she quipped, "As I always say, the price is right!"

That's not to say the school, which is about three-fifths white, lacks challenges. For one, there's a lot of self-segregation among the students, to which there seems to be no evident solution. This is particularly obvious at lunchtime. The school has an open campus policy, which means students are free to leave its grounds. Most of the affluent kids take advantage of this, abandoning the cafeteria to the students getting free lunch. But the stratification doesn't stop there. The McDonald's across the street from the school sees a fairly diverse lunch crowd, as its dollar menu attracts students of lesser means. But, Lockard explained, only the more affluent kids make the three-block trek to Chipotle, where a burrito bowl will cost you seven bucks.

Families notice this segregation. "The birthday parties are very integrated when they are little, and everybody's cute," Lockard said. "I know some parents who feel their black sons were not invited as they got older . . . The invitations just fell away."

The school also faces a glaring achievement gap. While 97 percent of its white students are proficient in math, just 78 percent of its African American students and 69 percent of its Hispanic students are. It's likely that these gaps are related to class as well as race—about a quarter of the school's black and Hispanic students receive a free or reduced-price lunch, and maybe twice that many are eligible. (Virtually none of B-CC's white students are poor enough to qualify.) Still, as in Shaker Heights, these low numbers also reflect middle-class minority students who are performing worse than their white peers.

Lockard is particularly worried about African American males, whose peer culture, she says, discourages academic achievement. To address the problem, the school holds an annual Minority Achievement Assembly that fills the auditorium. It starts with a video of B-CC kids of color addressing the audience and saying, for instance, "Hi, my name's Karen and I take AP lit and IB [International Baccalaureate] psychology." Lockard said, "We just roll the videotape. And you hear the kids saying, 'I didn't know he—he's a football player, I didn't know he was so smart!'" A few weeks later, when the kids register for classes, counselors strongly encourage them to sign up for Advanced Placement or International Baccalaureate courses—and to get their friends to sign up, too.

This full-court press toward challenging courses is a hallmark of B-CC, and of Montgomery County high schools in general. The district has an explicit goal of opening up advanced classes to more students, especially kids of color. The idea is that, with the right support, many more students have the aptitude to succeed in such courses than have traditionally signed up for them. The evidence is bearing this out. In 2005–06, for example, 19 percent of the school's African American graduates and 26 percent of its Hispanic graduates had earned at least a 3 out of 5, or "qualified to receive college credit," on an AP exam or the roughly equivalent IB score of 4. Just two years later, those numbers were up to 27 and 41 percent, respectively. Over the same period, passing rates for white students on those advanced exams went from 78 percent to 85 percent.

Such a rosy outcome wasn't a given when these reforms were first adopted. Understandably, both teachers and the parents of high-achieving students were worried that opening these courses to less-prepared students would water them down. This concern is hardly unique to B-CC; a 2009 national survey of AP teachers, for instance, found that almost two-thirds said they would like to see more screening of students to ensure that they are ready to do AP-level work.[5]

But administrators worked hard to get buy-in from parents and teachers, and also provided a lot of support to make sure the push for greater access didn't result in lower quality. That support was personified by Stacy Farrar, the school's staff development teacher. An energetic twenty-year veteran, Farrar bears a resemblance—in both looks and demeanor—to Katie Couric. As she'll tell you, "I have a great job." She's right. Her role is to work one-on-one with teachers to improve their practice. By all accounts she's very, very good at it.

Job number one for Farrar is to help teachers differentiate instruction. This only makes sense; now that somewhat weaker students are signing up for honors, AP, and IB courses, teachers are faced with the challenge of reaching a broader spectrum of kids. As we've discussed earlier, only the best teachers do this really well. Farrar's focus is on getting more of B-CC's teachers to that level.

I had an opportunity to see what this looks like up close. Farrar and I visited a ninth-grade honors biology course on a grey November day. The students looked sleepy (it was second period, not yet 9 a.m.) yet attentive. About twenty-five of them sat at laboratory tables spaced evenly around the room. Perhaps five or six of the students were kids of color.

Several of them likely wouldn't have been there just a few years earlier. That's when the science department still offered an on-level biology class. But there were just two sections of those—the rest were honors—and students in them were behaving and performing terribly. Those classes were also overwhelmingly minority. So the department decided to eliminate those sections and split all the on-level kids among the honors courses.

In many schools this would have resulted in mutiny from angry parents of mostly white high-achieving kids. But with Farrar's help, the teachers handled the transition well. And what I saw was remarkable, at least to my eyes. At first, the class seemed quite traditional. The teacher, Anne Merrell, gave a lesson on DNA and RNA. (It went right over my head.) To check students' understanding, she called on kids at random, by pulling index cards with their names on them. One student—an on-level kid, it turned out—gave a pretty good, if not sophisticated, answer when called. Then Merrell called on another student, an honors kid this time, to "extend" the answer. Now the class was having a discussion that seemed appropriate for freshman biology—freshman *college* biology.

After the short lesson, Merrell had the students work on an in-class assignment, to create an alien using the DNA/RNA process she had described. Here's when things got really nuanced. There were actually two different forms of the assignment. But that was apparent to me only after Farrar pointed it out. The students themselves probably didn't know, because the handouts for each assignment looked remarkably similar. But the honors assignment challenged students to handle a greater degree of ambiguity, while the on-level handout spelled things out in greater detail. Both expected students to learn the material at a reasonably high level, but the honors assignment went deeper.

With a mix like this, Merrell has to prepare two different lessons for each class, and teach them simultaneously. "It's really hard," she said. But in the hands of a gifted teacher—and with the support of someone like Farrar—it seems to be doable. As a result, B-CC continues to excel academically while also making the most of its rich diversity.

Private Schools: More Diverse than Public Schools?

You may think it ludicrous to look for diversity within private schools. Aren't they bastions of privilege, exclusive enclaves for the rich, white, and powerful? Perhaps that was so once upon a time, particularly during the heyday of desegregation, when many a "Christian Academy" sprung up to serve white kids fleeing the public schools. Now, however, the private school community embraces the goal of diversity. Patrick Bassett, the head of the National Association of Independent Schools, boasted to me that "you are more likely to find diversity in an independent school than a public school." The website of nearly any high-end independent school posts statements (and sometimes long essays) about the value of diversity and the school's commitment to it.

As we learned in Chapter One, there are clear educational benefits that accrue from a diverse school environment. Expensive private schools cater to parents who want their children well prepared for challenging colleges and twenty-first-century careers. These parents know their kids need to be ready for a multicultural America (and world). Going to an all-white school just won't do.

At the same time, America's growing ranks of upper-middle-class African American and Latino families are an attractive market niche for independent schools. Their children may, in turn, benefit mightily from private schools. Remember the Roland Fryer study on popularity and GPAs? The "Shaker Heights syndrome"—whereby black students are afraid to do well academically lest they become unpopular—disappears in private schools, probably because, as Fryer surmises, "blacks attending private schools have quite a different peer group."

But black and Latino parents will only choose private schools with a critical mass of students of color. Prestigious private schools, then, have a strong incentive to reach out and recruit a sufficiently diverse student body. That means attracting affluent black and Latino families, but also making scholarships available to minority pupils from poor or middle-class homes. Because private schools are not defined by specific geographic boundaries, they can attract these families from across a city or even a metropolitan area.

The best thing about diverse private schools, from a parent's perspective, is that they are low on risk and high on reward. (Of course, they are not low on cost!) While their students are diverse racially and sometimes socioeconomically, they are not diverse academically. Private schools can screen out students who are low-achieving or exhibit discipline problems, which makes an enormous difference.

I had a chance to talk about all of this with Richard Lodish, the head of the Sidwell Friends lower school in Washington, D.C. Lodish, who is white, is one of the main reasons that 40 percent of Sidwell's pupils (including the Obama daughters) are now kids of color. When he started at Sidwell decades ago, that number was 4 percent. But Lodish was committed to reaching out to minority communities to make the school a welcoming and inclusive place that lives up to its Quaker ideals. He himself had learned to live and work in racially integrated environments as a young man, first during college when he rented an apartment with black housemates in a mostly black community outside Pittsburgh, and then when he taught in inner-city Cleveland schools.

Lodish ended up at Sidwell somewhat by accident. "I don't like independent schools, basically," he admitted. "However, Quaker schools are different in many positive ways." Once there, he started going to black churches, community meetings—anywhere he could spread his message that parents of all races should consider Sidwell for their children. "I felt very comfortable," he told me. "You have to be real. Really feel people and know people. They have to know that they aren't just there for window dressing. You have to treat every person the way you would want to be treated."

He also set out to attract a diverse staff, and he's been successful on that front, too. Forty percent of the lower school's teachers are people of color, a rate that even diverse public schools would envy. Lodish went to "places that private schools don't usually recruit teachers from." But his standards were exacting. "You have to have the qualities of a great teacher," he said, "or you don't belong here."

I asked Lodish if a school like Sidwell offered parents the rewards of diversity without the risks. After saying that "nothing in life is risk free," he acknowledged, "Generally speaking, yeah." I probed further. Is there a racial achievement gap at Sidwell? "I can't honestly say. We don't look at that in great detail." Are there tensions around black underperformance or "acting white" or all the rest? "Very few that I'm aware of," he said.

Lowell School

The independent Lowell School serves 300 pre-Kindergarten to eighth-grade students on a leafy, fairy-tale campus hugging Rock Creek Park in Washington's Colonial Village neighborhood. Since its founding forty years ago, Lowell has prided itself on a commitment to racial diversity and inclusiveness. Sixteen percent of its students are African American, another 14 percent are multiracial, and 5 percent are Asian or Hispanic. (The school also keeps tabs on other demographic data: how many students are adopted, how many are raised by gay couples, and so on.)

I visited Lowell on a crisp, sparkling Tuesday in October, to join a weekly tour for prospective parents. It was a diverse bunch—a mix of white, black, Asian, and Latino men and women, several with international accents. Most of us were casually dressed, but one man with slicked-back hair wore a sharp suit and looked like your prototypical wheeler and dealer. Yet he was the one who seemed out of place; this private school definitely did not have a corporate boardroom feel.

As we walked the hallways, we could see brilliant red and orange leaves out of every window; handsome brick colonials and Tudors dotted the perimeter. What was happening inside the school was just as spectacular. Students were clustered into small classes of fifteen and led through engaging, creative lessons by smart, resourceful teachers. Everywhere you looked, there was art,

art, and more art. An exhibit of pointillism covered one hallway; it looked like the work of high school students but was the product of second graders. That's what happens when a school boasts three separate art galleries, not to mention a dance studio, science labs, music room, and more.

Lowell certainly passed the gut test; I could sense that this was a great school, with students engaged in meaningful, challenging, and joyful—yes, joyful—work.

After the tour, as I attempted to quash the feeling of intense longing for a school I could never afford, I sat down with Debbie Gibbs, the head of school, and Michelle Belton, the director of admissions and diversity. Gibbs, who is white, is a lifelong educator who started her career at the Blake School in Minneapolis, then moved to Marin County, California, where she was a teacher and administrator at another independent school. Belton is a stylish, youthful-looking African American woman who has been involved in several national and local efforts to make independent schools more diverse. She had been at the school since 1990—her daughters both attended when they were younger—and was leading the school's efforts to craft a new "diversity strategic plan."

As we sat in Gibbs's office, I asked how diversity plays out at Lowell. I started with the curriculum. It was obvious that the school embraced a progressive philosophy. (There were lots of hands-on activities, rote learning was downplayed, and the children called their teachers by their first names.) I understood why that might appeal to touchy-feely white parents, but was there a concern among African American parents about this approach?

"I would say yes," Belton replied quickly. "For families who did not grow up with progressive education as their background, which a lot of us have not, you do have to educate parents about what that means and what the gain is."

"We have to make it clear to people," Gibbs added, "that the kids [leave here] well-prepared. African American families, particularly with boys, are more worried because of the statistics that are out there. They are not blind. They get it. They are tracking what's going on in a different way. They may not care that 'adaptation' is this year's theme in second grade. But they care mightily whether we are keeping our faculty diverse. If something slips there, like someone leaves, which can happen, that will be a worry. 'Is the school committed to having role models that my child needs?'"

I asked if the school's diversity is a selling point to parents. "Sometimes that is the only reason they choose Lowell," Gibbs said about her white families. "They say, 'There are lots of schools with good programs.' It's the diversity that's a huge factor—the way we work with kids so the kids learn to be respectful within a diverse community. They also understand that the kind of critical thinking we are promoting requires that different perspectives be represented." As for the parents of color, Belton said, many are relieved to be able to spare their children their own experiences of being the only minority child in a class.

I noted that I hadn't seen any instances of self-segregation in the school. Kids of different races sat with each other at lunch, for example—was there really no racial tension at the school?

"We're not afraid to take things on," Gibbs said. "If something happens outside of school, or inside school, someone has done something that could be construed as racist, we won't shy away from it. We'll tackle the problem with the children in a developmentally appropriate way."

At the end of our meeting, Gibbs and Belton invited me to attend Lowell's upcoming "dialogue on race," where an official from the National Association of Independent Schools presented a survey instrument it had developed to help schools gauge their climate as it relates to diversity issues. That session, encouragingly, was well attended by a diverse group of parents, teachers, and board members.

Here's a place where the "common school" ideal lives on, where honoring diversity is a commitment, not just a slogan. Were it not for the $25,000 tuition, it could be a model for the nation.

Endnotes

1   Naomi Calvo, "How Parents Choose Schools: A Mixed-Methods Study of Public School Choice in Seattle" (doctoral dissertation, Harvard University John F. Kennedy School of Government, 2007).

2   Abigail and Stephan Thernstrom, *No Excuses: Closing the Racial Gap in Learning* (New York: Simon & Schuster, 2004), Chapter Seven.

3   John U. Ogbu and Astrid Davis, *Black American Students in an Affluent Suburb: A Study of Academic Disengagement* (Hoboken, NJ: Lawrence Erlbaum Associates, 2003).

4   Roland Fryer, "Acting White," *Education Next* 6, no. 1 (2006), 58.

5   Steve Farkas and Ann Duffett, *Growing Pains in the Advanced Placement Program: Do Tough Trade-Offs Lie Ahead?* (Washington, D.C.: Thomas B. Fordham Institute, May 2009).

Epilogue

A week after I finished the first draft of *The Diverse Schools Dilemma*, my wife gave birth to our second son, and the book project was put on the shelf. Soon, our little bungalow came to feel quite crowded. When our younger son turned one, we started to look for a new home.

We put our house on the market and were relieved when it sold a few weeks later. (This was the spring of 2011, and the housing market—even in recession-proof Washington, D.C.—was anemic.) Now the clock was ticking: We had about a month to put in an offer on a new house, which meant confronting the school question head-on. Were we going to stick with Takoma Park and its public schools, or were we going to bolt for greener pastures?

Even after researching and writing this book—or maybe because of it—I was still tied in knots. My head said that Takoma Park's diverse schools would be fine for my sons. If my wife and I continued to do our part at home, our kids would do okay anywhere. And Takoma's schools were better than okay: Mr. G. and the other educators were making a thoughtful effort to take advantage of their schools' rich diversity and to ensure that all students were challenged. The white students at Takoma Park's Piney Branch Elementary were outperforming the white students at virtually every other school in Montgomery County. And the teenagers we'd met who had gone through the school system were remarkable: mature, resilient, confident.

But my heart wasn't so sure. It couldn't shake that first impression of Piney Branch and its soulless design, institutional feel, and slightly chaotic culture. It didn't line up with my hopes and dreams for my sons' education. I wanted them at a place that was as joyful, warm, and loving as the Waldorf preschool where my older boy was enrolled. (Waldorf is a super-progressive, low-tech style of education that stresses relationships, creativity, and holistic learning—the kind of school, as we've learned, that many upper-middle-class parents say they want for their kids.) And the idea of one day sending my sons to the 3,000-student Montgomery Blair High School—our local school—frankly scared the hell out of me, what with its intimidating size and reputed gang presence.

So as we started looking for homes, we hedged. We set up a Redfin search for Takoma Park, but looked in other neighborhoods too. We liked Chevy Chase, with its beautiful old bungalows and Victorians, strollable shopping district, and real community feel. Its schools, including Bethesda-Chevy Chase High School, were great, and had some—but not too much—socioeconomic diversity. But it soon became apparent that if we wanted a bigger house, Chevy Chase was way out of our price range. Other appealing parts of Washington were much the same. With so many creative class Gen-Xers wanting to live in the city, walkable neighborhoods demanded a premium.

Affordable Takoma Park was looking more attractive again, but there was a problem. No bigger houses were coming on the market. So we started looking farther afield. We decided that if we couldn't have a cool, urban neighborhood, we'd at least want access to nature and a community swimming pool. We began to look at neighborhoods in western Bethesda, along the Potomac River, about twenty-five minutes from where we were living. One Saturday, the Redfin iPhone app directed my wife and me to a mid-century modern home perched high above the river. We peeked inside. (Since it was mostly glass, we could see a lot.) We fell in love with it, and decided to put in a lowball offer. The owners countered, and before we knew it, our bid was accepted.

Almost immediately, I had buyer's remorse. At every step in the process, I considered pulling out. Did I really want to move to Bethesda? Why were we leaving our friends in Takoma Park? What's more, my wife and I were coming to love the holistic, gentle Waldorf approach; Bethesda's public schools, on the other hand, are known for being college-prep pressure cookers.

In the middle of all of this craziness I thought to look and see which elementary school the house was zoned for. I couldn't believe it.

Wood Acres Elementary, the least diverse school in Montgomery County. You have to be kidding me!

■ ■ ■

As I write this, it's March 2012, and we've been in our new house for about nine months. Not a day goes by that I don't think about returning to Takoma Park. It's not that living in a beautiful glass house near the Potomac River is some kind of hardship. I have an amazing bike commute along a canal; the kids, now two and four years old, love riding their scooters in our cul-de-sac; we're a five-minute drive from another Waldorf preschool.

But I miss the sense of community that we left behind. I wonder about whether we could go back and make the Takoma Park schools work for us. Or maybe we could afford to live in Takoma Park and send our kids to the Lowell School and have the best of all worlds: a great community and a great, diverse school for our kids.

So how is this story going to end? Chances are, we'll grow more accustomed to our new environs, make new friends, and find a new sense of community. One of our neighbors, whose children are now grown, went through this two decades ago. She cried for three years, she told me, after leaving the city for the suburbs. But her kids had a wonderful experience and are now thriving. "I became an adult when I moved here," she told me. "It was the first time in my life I made a decision based on what was best for someone else than for me."

I'm still not sure what's best for us, or for our kids. We'll give the leafy suburbs a try. But watch out, Takoma Park, because we might be back before you know it.

Acknowledgments

Birthing this book took three years, start to finish, and couldn't have been done without the support and encouragement from a multitude of people for whom I feel a great amount of gratitude. First and foremost is my wife Meghan, who allowed me to chronicle our own family's journey through the diverse schools dilemma, provided great feedback on an early draft, and brought much wisdom to the project as a talented educator and mother.

Also essential were the trustees of the Thomas B. Fordham Institute, in particular its president (and my boss and mentor) Chester (Checker) Finn, who allowed me to take a three-month "mini-sabbatical" in the fall of 2009 to research and write the book. Checker also lent his enormous editorial talents to shaping up an early draft.

He was far from alone. Several friends and colleagues looked at manuscripts along the way and provided essential guidance and improvements including Alan Berube, Ulrich Boser, Jamie Davies-O'Leary, Chris Doherty, Pete Ford, Kalman Hettleman, Andre and Melissa Javier-Berry, Richard Kahlenberg, Robert Pondiscio, and Marty West. Linda Perlstein, author and editor extraordinaire, tightened a final manuscript into a crisper, sharper final product. (Linda would have encouraged me to delete "sharper" because it's duplicative, and she's a stickler about using as few words as possible. Thank you for that, Linda!)

I'm also indebted to all of the scholars, educators, parents, and activists I interviewed for the book. Rick Kahlenberg was particularly helpful and generous with his time as I studied the literature on school desegregation.

The team at Fordham has been incredibly supportive and helpful too—including in covering for me when I was out on sabbatical or working on the final manuscript. Janie Scull provided much research assistance in the early months of the project and shepherded the book to completion in its latter months. An army of interns helped me pull up research findings, relevant articles, and more: Jack Byers, Daniela Fairchild, Marisa Goldstein, Kyle Kennedy, Saul Spady, Jessica Klein, Amanda Olberg, Remmert Dekker, Marena Perkins, Gerilyn Slicker, Josh Pierson, Alicia Goldberg, Laura Johnson, Michael Ishimoto, Layla Bonnot, and Lisa Gibes. Joe Portnoy is responsible for the wonderful cover image and jacket design, and Tyson Eberhardt and Stephen Manfredi for its marketing. Roger Williams served as copyeditor and Alton Creative, Inc. as layout designer.

One and all: Thank you.

About the Author

Michael J. Petrilli is one of the nation's foremost education experts. He is executive vice president of the Thomas B. Fordham Institute, a think tank focused on K-12 education policy, and also an executive editor of the journal *Education Next*. Petrilli has published opinion pieces in the *New York Times*, *Washington Post*, and *Wall Street Journal* and appears regularly on *NBC Nightly News*, *ABC World News Tonight*, CNN, and Fox. He's been a guest on several National Public Radio programs, including *All Things Considered*, *Talk of the Nation*, and *The Diane Rehm Show*. He is author, with Frederick M. Hess, of *No Child Left Behind: A Primer*. Previously, Petrilli was an official in the U.S. Department of Education. He lives with his wife and two sons in the Washington, DC area.